The Serving Church:

When it's not about you, it can be about Him

by Paul Alan Clifford

Copyright information

If you would like to invite the author to speak at an event for your organization, please contact him via email or the website.

Advanced praise:

Paul Clifford wrote "This is a story about an ordinary guy who honestly believes that his life has to be about others." If you are a Christian that has a heart to reach others for God, then this book will surely touch you. The author is down to earth, genuine, and honestly transparent.

On page three of the last chapter, "Serving Outside the Church," he wrote, "It made me cry." Reading that part caused me to cry too - for myself - because he was describing me. I was convicted and felt ashamed for my ungiving and unserving attitude. The end of the previous chapter had also prepared me for those tears to come.

I really enjoyed it because he says what I feel. Just to hear it expressed motivates and encourages me. I highly recommend this book!

Charles Windham

"This isn't anyone's ministry except the Lord's. We need to all remember that in our interactions with each other. We're all on the same team, trying to see lives and eternities changed; let's act like it."

Paul does a great job of addressing our responsibility to "Serve the Church" as well as what it means to be a "Serving Church." The majority of church attendees want to be fed and rarely take on the challenge of what it means to actually "Be the Church."

Hearing about service from the view of a layperson and not a professional staff members, makes the message more impactful. This is not another bashing of those who are not serving but a call to action of how we are most like Christ when we make serving part of our everyday lives. Each of us, as members of the Body of Christ, has an area of gifting and should be looking for ways to use our gifts to serve.

"Put this book down and take one small step into something that helps others."

"What little step can you take today to help someone else?"

This book is a great resource for pastors, missionaries, and volunteer leaders to take and share with their teams and use when training volunteers on the benefits of service.

Darrell West

In recent years, we have been seeing more and more books about serving in your faith through your church. Many, if not most, of these books are written from the perspective of a "professional church" person, either a pastor or missions director of a local church. While there are many good thoughts being printed from that perspective, we don't see a lot from the perspective of the average church goer.

Paul Clifford decided to change that. While he does work with churches in his "day" job, this book is written from his view as a committed volunteer in his local church. The theology and thought process are solid which means that pastors, mission directors, etc. will find some good background material here, but it is the refreshing view from underneath that makes this book a gem for me.

It is, oh so easy, to assume that people will latch on to what you are saying about serving as a Christian, it is another thing to hear what it means to be on the receiving end of these sermons and exhortations and to see the commitment of average churchgoers as they go about serving.

Overall, well done and a pleasant read.

Roger A Vest

Dedication

To my wife Christina who's put of with a lot of trouble as I pursue my dream to help churches. Someday I hope I can serve my bride as effortlessly as I serve Jesus' bride.

To my daughters Trinity and Eliana. I hope you continue to learn how great a selfless life is. I wouldn't hesitate to die to keep you safe.

To my God who showed me that selfishness leads to sadness and selflessness leads to joy. Father God, You gave Your Son. Jesus, You gave Your life. Holy Spirit, You gave all inspiration that every artist has ever depended on for their creativity.

Table of Contents

Introduction

"Daddy, how can I serve tomorrow if Mommy and Ellie are at home?" My then 10-year-old looked at me with a genuine look of distress on her face. She'd just found out that her little sister was sick. Her mother would be staying home instead of going to my church's campus in Frankfort, KY, as usual. Our church has a program that lets interested fifth and sixth graders help with leading younger kids.

There are some things that warm your heart to the core. Maybe it's your child's smile or the excited words, "Daddy's home!" when you're the last home from work in the evening. For me, it was what she said in response to what I said next. "Well, I guess you could come with me when I leave at 6:00

tomorrow morning." A look of relief came over her face. "Can I? That would mean that I could serve in KidsQuest!"

Trinity loves to sleep and, like many kids her age, can sometimes be dramatic when she's not perfectly rested. The next morning, she was neither cranky nor lethargic. I leave over an hour before my wife and daughters do, so I didn't know what to expect from my firstborn. She was amazing.

I serve tirelessly on the weekends because I know what goes on in the background. I see lives and eternities change when I sacrifice my time and preferences. I didn't know if she had the eyes to see what I see, but she did. Even recounting the story now, I feel the tears of pride welling up inside me as all the mistakes I've made as a parent seem not to matter in this one case. My eldest daughter would rather lose sleep and be inconvenienced than let her role go unfilled. That's huge for me to know.

Why *The Serving Church*? This is my fourth book. I've written three church technology books, now: *Podcasting Church*, *Tweeting Church*, and *Church Video Summer School*. You might think that I'd stick with the technology theme, but I'm taking this side trip on purpose.

There is something odd about me. I don't know why, but things that are hard for others are assumed for me. You might have missed what I said earlier about my normal Sunday morning schedule. I get up sometime in the fives and head forty miles away from my house to be the first person at my church's Frankfort campus. I've done this for almost four years now. I've missed a few weeks, maybe ten to twelve, but I'm almost always there. We have a morning practice that starts between 7:00 and 7:30, a run- through at 8:15 for our 9:30 service and another service at 11:30. Oh, and I'm a volunteer.

I guess that's important for a lot of pastors that don't think people like me exist. I do. Through the week, I work as a church technology consultant (with various degrees of success), but the church doesn't pay me a dime. Part of why I'm writing this book is that I've read books by Christian leaders that I trust, but I don't see any by people like me, down in the trenches, making ministry happen, despite the stereotypes of pew-warmers or "the frozen chosen." I guess I just want to spread a virus of sorts to people who might be thinking they're too busy, as well as to pastors who think that no one has a selfless attitude anymore.

I'm excited about the possibility that maybe, just maybe, we'll see a groundswell of people who think, like I do, that I'm a temporary resident here on Earth. I don't know how long I have; I could live for another eighty years or die in a few minutes. I just know that my house doesn't come with me when I die and neither do my car, my camera, or my laptop.

Only the people whose trajectory has been affected by our small actions, following the nudges from the Holy Spirit, come with us.

I toyed with calling this book *The Doulos Manifesto* (*doulos* is Greek for a type of slave and what the Apostle Paul often called himself) or *It's Not About You*, but in the end, I didn't come to believe these things in a vacuum. Community has been vital in shaping me into the man I am today, imperfect as I am. That's why this isn't a story about me (although my experiences are the lens through which I'll speak), but the story of a church where I'm learning more and more that my life isn't lost when I give it away; it's multiplied into the lives of people.

I hope that's what comes across as I write. I hope that all the talk you hear about how the American Church is headed in the wrong direction is tempered, if only just a little, by the story of an ordinary guy who lives somewhere outside of Lexington, KY, and who honestly believes that his life has to be about others.

1. The Why Behind the What

Why can't I be content with a life that's normal? Why am I always striving for more? Maybe it started before I was even born. My parents thought they couldn't have kids. They were married for eighteen years and from what my mother has told me, they did nothing to prevent pregnancy after their first year or so (that's really all the details I want to know). So what happened in those seventeen years that kept me from having older brothers and sisters? I don't know absolutely. Sometimes it seems like it just becomes the right time for things to happen. In early 1973, my mother got pregnant. My father was in his late forties and my mother in her late thirties. They wanted children, so they were ecstatic.

From as early as I can remember, my parents both told me that I was here for a reason. My life was on purpose. God had a plan specifically for me. There were so many reasons that I shouldn't be here that I needed to take hold of the gift of life and use it.

The pattern of waiting patiently for God's plan started before I was born, but has continued on since. I became a Christian in November of 1982, but I still didn't see the purpose of my life, even though I knew that I had one. Things started to roll into focus twenty-five years ago. The trajectory of my life changed when I heard Jesus tell me that He wanted my life to be used for His service and not my plans. I couldn't imagine myself in a traditional church role, so I was still unclear about the details, but I said yes to whatever the plan was.

I went through several plans during college, but each seemed wrong for me somehow. I wanted to be a Christian musician, but really lacked the talent for that. I was good at philosophy, but it wasn't quite right, either. Seminary seemed like the obvious next step, but the one I chose was a poor fit for my theological perspective. Finally, I landed at Asbury Seminary in Wilmore, KY. There I found a school that matched what I believed and which had classes in a subject that I'd dismissed as irrelevant to my ministry call -- technology.

When I took classes in video, the world seemed to open to me. This form of expression made it possible for me to share my heart in a way that connected with people in our culture. I was surprised to find a conjunction of my love of video and love of Jesus. I just needed a place to serve in this area.

While taking a class called "Servant as Leader," I was introduced to the church that would become my church — Quest Community Church. I remember being amazed that adults were becoming Christians at this church. Almost immediately after we started attending, my wife and I befriended another couple who was clearly on the road toward faith. I remember telling her that I couldn't believe that in a few weeks it actually looked like these new friends would come to know Jesus. During the series "The Truth about Being a Christian" in early 2001, that's exactly what happened.

At a restaurant after the service, I was given a gift that had me literally on my knees. I'd been on the video team for a few months and had done a lot of the work behind the video that we'd used in our first series of the year. It was for the series "Navigating the Storms of Life." When asked about what had precipitated his decision to come to Christ, a guy named Jim that I'd never met, "That storms of life video was so real that I started to see that I really needed Jesus." When I heard those words for the first time, I collapsed. I don't mean I was breathless or that I wasn't feeling good. I mean I briefly lost control of my legs and caught myself before I hit the ground. I remember thinking, "The Lord God of the universe used me. He used me. I didn't even know what I was doing, but I helped make something clear to Jim that wasn't clear before." Twelve years later as I sit writing about it, the tears are flowing down my cheeks as I remember the power of that moment.

Sometimes my role has been small and almost by accident. Sometimes I've intentionally sought out a person who I knew needed to know Jesus. Whatever it was, I was a part of a team that helped change lives and eternities. I'm no one special. I had nothing to do with being born to parents who raised me to believe that I was here for a reason. I just chose to say yes to the call of Christ on my life.

Now, some twelve years after I started going to my church, I'm convinced that serving churches don't just happen. You have to know why you're doing hard things to do them. I've got enough trust in the bank for my leaders that when I don't see why, I do what I can anyway. I know that somehow it leads to lives and eternities changing.

It's really all about perspective. If you look at the hard things in your circumstances, like not having enough money, being busy, etc., and you don't see what God's doing, it will be very hard. If you can connect the dots from what you're doing to something amazing that God is doing, your part, no matter how small, is significant.

My pastor loves football metaphors, so I'm going to use one in homage to him. Imagine you work for a football team. You aren't on the field; you're not the coach. You're a water boy (or girl). You could easily get caught up in how unimportant you feel. You're not the quarterback and you're not the coach; you're not even on the field at all. Anyone could do what you do. But not just anyone is. You get to hand water to the people that are making the big plays happen and are winning the game. They could literally die if you didn't show up. Being the keeper of the water is important when you see the whole.

Likewise, look at what you get to do (more about that later) at church. How small is it really? Do you pick up trash or do you help welcome newcomers with a clean environment? Do you change dirty diapers or do you provide peace of mind to new parents that their precious babies are taken care of so that they can be in the service without being distracted? Do you just click buttons on a computer or do you enable people to feel at home in a church service because they can sing along with the songs and not feel like outcasts? You really are important to what God is doing at your church. Look for it and embrace it.

I don't know what your "why" is, but you need to. Knowing a big "why" is how I can serve tirelessly. It's what gets me through hard times. Your "why" has to be bigger than "they seem to need me" or "I like babies." Think about what's big enough to get you through disappointment, hurt feelings, fatigue, or whatever could cause you to quit. You're needed; I can say that for sure. Just get a clear picture of your big "why" and it will help keep you doing what you're supposed to do when it's tough.

2. Get to and Have to

I was at our church's leadership Christmas party a few years ago. I started to notice that something was different. People had removed a phrase and replaced it with another. It was very simple, but profound. I kept hearing people say "get to" where people would normally say "have to." It went something like "I'll be at church early tomorrow. I get to run the video in the morning."

Let's look at the same sentence the normal way. "I'll be at church early tomorrow. I have to run the video in the morning." Do you see the difference between these two? One is obligation and the other is privilege. If you look at everything you go through as a something that's a privilege, it changes how you view it.

I think this is what the Apostle Paul was saying in 2 Corinthians 4:17-18 when he said, "For our light and momentary troubles are achieving for us an eternal glory that far outweighs them all. So we fix our eyes not on what is seen, but on what is unseen, since what is seen is temporary, but what is unseen is eternal." Clearly his troubles were much more pressing than mine. I've never been whipped for my faith. I've never been stoned (in either sense, but here I'm talking about the Biblical, with rocks,` kind). Having a stretch in my finances or waking up a little early isn't really a big deal.

It's really easy to be a complainer. Don't hear me say that it isn't. Anything less than your expectations can move you from happiness, to frustration, to complaining, and even to anger. Don't feel bad if that's your pattern; do something about it.

Here's the challenge. Can you replace "have to" with "get to?" This might seem like a little exercise, but I really think that it can impact who you are and even change a culture if it becomes the norm.

There's a similar idea I heard once that I hope will guide you. What if instead of asking "why me," we asked "why not me?" This seems like a trite phrase, but the person I heard it from had a child with developmental issues. This was his response to a situation that would cause many people to curse God or shake their fists in anger (and I wish I could remember who he is to give him credit).

It's easy to start believing that God has promised us security and happiness, but I really don't see that anywhere in the Bible, at least not in an earthly way. Jesus promised that we **would** have trouble and He promised not to leave us. Do you think that Jesus messed up His mission, and that's why His life ended so badly on the cross? What about Stephen? Was he living a wonderful life filled with easy choices and following simple steps when he was killed? Did the twelve apostles all live long lives into retirement, where they passed away peacefully in their sleep, surrounded by family, or were they all killed except for John, who died in exile? As far as we can tell from the Bible they all had hard lives where their perspective was that it's better to suffer and have Jesus than to live a perfect life without Him.

So, why do we act like hard things are a surprise? A hard life is expected by most people in most of the world, and yet I've complained when I had to change the batteries in the remote to my television. I've never gone without in the same way that people during the Great Depression did, but I've pushed food away saying, "that's disgusting" to something that would be welcomed in a time of need.

I'm not saying any of these things to give you a guilt-trip or to say I'm better than you, because I'm not. I still have temper tantrums like a spoiled two-year-old when things don't go my way. I get mad at the people I love for imagined slights and offenses. I dream of a perfect life where I don't have problems and where my family knows how brilliant I am. Why? I do this all because I'm broken.

Broken people make a lot of mistakes. We know we need a Savior because all our best efforts to fix ourselves have failed. Sometimes, just sometimes we get the gift of changing something. Changing that something changes more than we'd think.

I was unemployed four months after that Christmas party when our church hosted its first conference. I stayed late one day and did work on the videos for the next day, burning DVDs for an announcement loop and just doing what I do. I was in the office with Robbie, my church's staff technical director. As I was completing my work after a long day, my pastor stopped by to talk to Robbie. He asked, "Paul, what are you still doing here?" I responded, "I get to be." He smiled and walked away.

So, what do you get to do? What's the hard thing in your life that's happening not because of a sin, a mistake, or even human frailty, but because you're called to it? Somehow, it seems we get a choice as to whether we agree with God's plans or fight them. Just because it's hard doesn't mean it's not God's will. Hard things sometimes come with the territory, so expect them.

When I look at history, I don't think of the people who had it easy as people who stepped into the plans God had for their lives. It's those that had hard lives, but who embraced their calling, that are the heroes of the faith. Martin Luther, John Wycliffe, Mother Teresa, and many others had lives filled with challenges.

Like anything, having a "get to" attitude takes practice. Very few people go to bed one night cursing mismatched socks and wake up to take on the role of patient saint the next. This is the process that theologians call "sanctification." Jesus slowly remakes us into the image of who we were always meant to be, but we have to choose it.

These choices might start really small, but little choices grow into bigger ones. I think of it this way: Jesus talked in the parable of the talents about being faithful with a little and then getting more. I think that's exactly the model we should pursue. Can you see a traffic jam as an opportunity to grow your patience? Can you see the nightly news reports of violent crimes as a time to love your enemies?

Our responsibility is to discern and follow God's will. You can choose that life, one that echoes in eternity, or you can choose a more mundane existence where you do what you want and play it safe, complaining about little inconveniences as they arrive.

I get to choose the former. I get to have challenges that I see no way past. I get to be the man God has called me to be even when it's hard, and I get to ignore the pettiness of my own preferences. I hope you'll get to join me in the hard things, seeing the Lord's hand in them. Will you? I believe the answer is up to you.

3. The Marine Principle

"It's no big deal. You arrive before the meeting, set it up. After the meetings end, you show up and tear it all down again. You're only really working for a 1/2 hour at a time. This is a really flexible job." The voice on the phone ended his sales pitch telling me why I should come to work for the company that he worked for.

I thought to myself, "This is the perfect job for me. I need something flexible enough that I can come and go as needed to serve at church." I was in.

It wasn't long after I started that I learned the reality. It **was** a big deal. It seemed that each group having a meeting, believed their business rose or fell based on how the audio and video worked. Over and over again, I'd set up a

17

room with something simple like a microphone, and someone would somehow find a way to cause it to malfunction. I'd get a call during church for a meeting where the stage people had unplugged the microphone from the wall while moving the stage. Two weeks later I'd get a panicked call with the same problem, and someone had just turned off the mic switch. I resolved to leave the job because it was much worse than I'd agreed to.

Don't soft-sell the vision. Don't tell people that something is easy when it's hard. That's the mistake my manager made when he hired me. He said it was easy, but it wasn't. As a result of what he told me, I could have come to two conclusions — that he wasn't honest with me and was trying to make the job more palatable, or that I was inadequate to the job. Knowing that this manager was the consummate salesman who would say whatever was necessary to close a sale, I chose the former. This really isn't what you want people in your care and under your leadership to wonder.

Contrast this to what happens if you get someone to join your cause when you've told them it's hard. It's hard to adequately tell how hard something is, but let's just say that you overemphasize the hard parts. What's your motivation for doing this? You don't want someone to think they're getting into something that's easy and regret it when it gets hard. You want them to be committed to the task at hand. If they find it hard, you warned them and they'll thank you for not lying about it. If they find it easier than anticipated, they'll have two options in considering why you told them it was harder than it is — you didn't want them to commit unless they were really ready, or they are better at the skill or activity than most people. This seems to be a "win/win" to me.

You don't get people who aren't really committed; they won't be testing the waters. You don't join a team that's hard if you don't really want to be there. They get to feel good about themselves when they find out that they've hit their stride.

This is why I call it "The Marine Principle." They don't recruit for the Marines by saying anything like, "Hey, no big deal. Anyone can be a Marine. It's a lot like camp. We even roast marshmallows." They say, "The Few, the Proud, the Marines." I've known a few Marines in my time, and they are people who don't back down easily. I know that if I'm ever in a hard situation with one of them, they're not going to say, "I'd rather go watch TV" and abandon me when I need them. That's the kind of person you want on your team.

When I'm recruiting for my team, I tell them the truth about it. "It's going to be hard. Every Wednesday, we have a practice from 7:00 until as late as 11:00 or midnight. I cut video every Saturday night after the service. Sometimes I'm there really late. Once or twice, I haven't gone home at all. The next morning, I wake up early and go to Frankfort. I'm the first one there. I get everything set up for practice, which lasts from 7:00 until right before the 9:30 service. When that gets done, I do it again. Then I take the recordings from the camera, start them compressing, and leave to have Will upload them. Finally, I drive home and take a nap. That's my week. I want your help to make that happen because I know that people's lives and eternities change because of what I do. I'm not asking you to join me every week, but can you do once a month?" If I can get someone to say yes after that, that person is committed.

Notice that I started with what I do every week. I don't ask them for more than I'm already doing. I show what can be done and set them up for success by telling them it's hard. I also say, "I think you can do this. You're the one to try. I believe in you." I mean that part. I'm not going to ask someone who can't do it. I don't say "no" for them, but I don't say to a 15 year-old, "hey, be here at 7:00 on Sunday morning" because he can't drive there to meet me. If I know that someone has a lot of last minute business trips, my team might not be the best fit either. Be wise in asking people who can do it, but don't say it's easy when it's not.

I have one other caution about calling people into a hard area of service. Some people will embrace a hard area because they want to get recognized, or they think they must work hard for God for it to somehow count. These are people to avoid until these attitudes have shifted. I don't want someone arriving early, staying late, or shouldering a heavy load spiritually if they're just trying to show how good a person they are. That's the wrong motivation for serving. Service has to come from the overflow of your relationship with Jesus.

Think about it this way: if I felt that I had to clean the house, wash the dishes, and fold all the laundry in order for my wife to love me, how long would it be until I became disgusted and quit if we had a fight? I might think, "I did all this stuff and now she's mad at me? The deal's off. It's not worth the work." If, in contrast, I love her and notice that she needs help with the things she does around the house, I might do the dishes just because I love her. It doesn't matter how she reacts (or how I perceive her to react); it's just a result of my love.

That's why I want you to avoid people who serve out of duty or a desire to be noticed. If they agree to serve, when it's hard, they're going to burn out. It's not a matter of if, but when.

I've done this for over a decade and when my pastor asks for difficult things, I don't resent it. I look forward to it. I know it matters. It's a gift to me that I get to do hard things because it means the results matter. I hope you and your team will feel the same.

4. Being a Steward

I have a confession to make. When I was in my teens, I wanted people to not understand me. I don't mean that I wanted to do things that didn't make sense, but that I wanted to have such a command of the English language that I'd purposely and unnecessarily use big words. Anyone listening wouldn't be able to understand what I meant, but would be impressed by my brilliance. That's in the past, though, because I realized that it defeated the purpose of communicating. Words have meaning only when both the speaker and the listener know what they mean.

In a past job, I worked with someone who hadn't learned this lesson. If a one-syllable word would work, he'd use a two-syllable or longer word. We had a piece of equipment that was built using a new method so that it wasn't really compatible with an older piece. Every time an installer would call to ask why they didn't work together, he'd say "[Piece A] isn't applicable for usage with [piece b]." I never got why he said "applicable for usage" when the phrase "doesn't work with" would work just as well and be understood more easily.

I think, in the church, we do the same thing. We're not trying to get people to recognize our brilliance, but recognize holiness. I'm just not sure it communicates what we want it to. Are we trying to feel more intelligent or communicate God's truth?

One of the words we use is "steward." I'll be honest: when I was a kid, I thought the word was "Stewart," and it meant there was some guy that was really good at watching out for people's stuff. He was so good at it that we started talking about other people being like him.

That's not the case. The word isn't used in our language very often, except maybe when you're reading the *Lord of the Rings* trilogy or when you talk about the person who takes care of the wine at a fancy restaurant.

Imagine stewardship on an x-y grid. There are people you'd trust for a short time with your kids. There are those you'd trust with your stuff for a short time. There are those you'd trust with your stuff for a long time. There are those you'd trust to raise your kids as their own and manage your estate.

I think there are four words that illuminate this idea for how you should treat your ministry, time, and resources. Let's start with **babysitter.** When you're a parent, you recognize from the moment your child takes her first breath that she will need a constant stream of care until her teens. I have two daughters. I told you about Trinity in the introduction. As I'm writing, she's 11. Eliana is 5. Last summer, I was working at home, so I was always around, but I needed to accomplish stuff. I decided that I'd employ Trinity to watch Ellie during the day. Basically, I paid her to play with her sister. This meant I could write *Church Video Summer School.* Trinity loves her sister, but I'm her dad. Trinity isn't Ellie's mom; my wife Christina is. Trin can keep her sister occupied, but I wouldn't trust her yet to watch Ellie for a week like I would my wife (and she would me).

I think a person can be a steward and not be much more than a babysitter. They don't have much invested in what they're caring for, but they do it and do it well. Part of the advantage to them of being a babysitter is that they can go home at the end of the day and not think about it.

There's another level to being a sitter though. Some people can take it to the point where the parents would trust them for a longer time. Miss Kathleen is that type of sitter. Every year when our church has our leadership retreat and we're gone for at least two and sometimes three days, she's our go-to person. The girls love her and she loves them. I wouldn't have a problem letting her watch them for as long as a couple of weeks if my wife and I were away on a trip.

The *babysitter level 2*, for lack of a better term, is someone whom you trust with dear things for much longer. They're much more responsible and can handle most problems, should they arise. A babysitter at this level is certainly closer to the family and loved almost like a member of it. They really understand the importance of their actions.

In the quadrant of someone whom you'd trust with your stuff, there's the **caretaker**. Maybe it's a maintenance person, a property manager, or someone similar. You know that they're there for the paycheck, but you trust them enough to know they're not likely stealing from you. They go home at the end of the day, happy the work is done. They might try to see how they can help in the case of an emergency, but they're not risking their lives.

You can be this type of person in your service. You get "paid" somehow in your church, not necessarily in money, but maybe in satisfaction or in the knowledge that you're helping out. If the church is burning, you might help make sure people don't go in, but you're not headed inside the burning building yourself. You're not willing to die (literally or metaphorically) for the ministry.

Trustees are like the babysitter level 2. They have more stake in the runnings of an organization. They understand what's at risk more. At this level, someone will sometimes put themselves at risk, to a point, to help the organization. My wife managed an apartment complex that was having financial difficulties. She showed that she was more than just a caretaker by being willing to delay her paycheck for a while to help the company succeed. She had a stake in the company that was more than financial; she believed in the owner.

You can serve at this level too. Do you sometimes buy things for the church when you know money is tight and "forget" to turn in the receipt for reimbursement? Have you ever arrived early or stayed late so that what needed to be done could be? Have you ever put what you'd prefer aside so that the kingdom of God could take steps forward? These are the actions of a trustee. Unfortunately, this is the highest level that most people are willing to serve at.

I think there's one more level. The final level is the level a **guardian** or **adoptive parent**. If something were to happen to my wife and me, there's one couple that I'd trust with our daughters. They're more than just long-term babysitters. I'd trust them to care for whatever we left financially for our daughters, as well as loving them and caring for them as their own. I think they'd raise them like we would.

Your service can be like that. Do you treat the ministry you're a part of like it's your own? Will you give of yourself and your preferences for what you're called to do? I'm not saying you should sacrifice yourself for a list of responsibilities. That's not why the disciples died. They died to safeguard the Church, Jesus' bride. Look at this as the opportunity to be the guardian for His bride. Would you put your reputation on the line for the bride of Christ and the work He assigned for us to do? In Acts 20:24, the Apostle Paul said, "However, I consider my life worth nothing to me, if only I may finish the race and complete the task the Lord Jesus has given me – the task of testifying to the gospel of God's grace." Those are the words, not of a babysitter, a caretaker, or a trustee, but of a guardian. That's who I want to be.

5. Having Flex in your Knees

There are phrases and sayings that develop in subcultures, but which need translation into others. "Having flex in your knees" is one of those. It's really easy to get into a rut, to be happy doing things your preferred way, but that's the enemy of almost every form of creativity and innovation. The world prizes these two for their own sake, but to me they're only tools.

Maybe you've seen *Fiddler On the Roof* and the song called "Tradition" is playing in your head right now. I'm not trying to say that tradition is evil or has no place in a serving church. Instead, I mean that sometimes we can make ourselves slaves to patterns that we don't need to stay in.

I once heard someone say that the words that mark the beginning of the death of a church are, "We've never done it that way before." On some level, that's true. If you're more concerned about being comfortable and keeping your kingdom safe, then there's no room for God's plans and His desire to expand His Kingdom.

"Having flex in your knees" means being both able and willing to change what needs to change for the sake of the Lord's Kingdom at the expense of your own desires and comfort. Is your church, your ministry, and your time about you, meant for and designed for you, or is it all about Jesus? When I say this, I mean it. I'm tired of hearing story after story of kingdoms (notice the little "k") inside churches where a certain person can't be offended because they might just snap and derail the plans of God.

I come to this feeling honestly. I was in seminary the first time I was part of a church where someone didn't like how ministry was being done. I did all I could to stop it, when a church member said she wanted *her* church back. She was reacting to the people who were coming to know Jesus, who weren't "respectable" or "dignified" enough for *her* church. Every sentence I heard from her lips was dripping with "me" and "mine." The poison of her self-centeredness oozed onto all she touched. I hated every moment of it.

God's love requires us to put our own agendas and preferences aside for the sake of others. I do this quite often. I love rock and rap, but as a kid raised in the church, I love hymns as well. Church isn't about me though. It's about Jesus. I think He's most glorified when we do what He did — seek and save the lost. That almost always means that we need to put our own preferences aside.

I've told you that the ministry I'm called to is technology. You might think that's why I'm so keen on change. It isn't. Technology is just a tool that enables us to reach more people and do it more easily. Technology is often confused with electronics, but it isn't true. Technology is any change or invention. The book is a technology that was quickly embraced by the church, replacing the scroll, because it enabled Scripture to be more easily concealed (from persecuting authorities), and also enabled non-linear access to certain parts of the Bible that were hard to get to before. A ball point pen enables writing more easily than a quill and inkwell. These are changes that make things easier.

Change shouldn't be for its own sake though. Change should serve the mission of the Church. Tradition isn't any good for its own sake either. Tradition should serve the mission of the Church. Do you see? Helping people to know Jesus so that they can become transformed into people who reach the lost is what matters more than hymns or rap.

Sometimes in a church service, being flexible in big ways is assumed, but it's the little ways that are harder. Can I turn on a dime to drop a song? Am I willing to put in a little more time at the last minute to help make the service communicate Jesus more clearly? It's like saying, "I'd die for You, Lord!" and not being willing to help someone cross the street. It's in the little things that your true feelings about the larger ones are revealed.

I'm not advocating arriving every Sunday with no plan, no practice, and winging it. I'm saying that sometimes last minute changes in what you were planning are necessary. I firmly believe that the Holy Spirit, being a member of the Trinity, knows what's going to happen long before we do. Sometimes artistic people, like myself, blame lack of planning on Him, as if The Holy Spirit got the last minute plans from the Father, who forgets to tell anyone what He's planning until the day of. That's nonsense. I'm not sure where the idea came from that the Holy Spirit only does stuff off the cuff. I don't see it in Scripture anywhere.

Still, sometimes we don't hear what He's saying, we decide we know better, or He conceals it from us for good reasons. In those cases, it really matters if you trust your leaders and are able to shift things. Sometimes what we didn't plan works better than what we did. This isn't to say that you shouldn't plan or blame failures in execution on the

Spirit either. Always do your best and prepare as best as you can, but roll with unforeseen circumstances.

Attitude matters too. Giving the children's pastor grief because he needs you to step into the four-year-old room instead of the first grade room isn't having flex in your knees. Complaining every moment that you're running the coffee maker, when you like setting out the Bible verses, isn't having a servant's heart. There are no little jobs in the Church. Don't treat it like there are. Remember what I said in an earlier chapter about connecting the dots. Do it. Realize how you're helping Jesus.

In order to be willing to be flexible, you have to have margin in your service. It might be really engaging to run full throttle all the time, but if something comes up, you may not be able to deal with it. I'm realizing more and more that we all have margin in our lives that we don't know about. We're all busy, but have you noticed that some people seem to be able to make time to do what they want to while others seem unable to do so? I think that comes from just being able to know what can be put off and what can't. My front yard looks horrible right now. That's because I've put it off to write. In your serving role, try to have the margin, or at the very least, the knowledge of what can be put off, so that you can do what's necessary when it's necessary.

It also matters who is asking for a change. I was directing the video at our church one night during practice. One of the girls from the tech team told me that my shots were off. I don't proudly state that I can't be wrong and move on. I'm always trying to better what I do, but after consideration, I didn't think she was right. Had the same request have come from our worship pastor, I would have embraced it as true immediately. Why? The source matters as much as the request. Sometimes you'll get a request that's a suggestion, but not really all that important.

Consider what you have before you act. Let people know what's involved. They might not want you to change, given the information you know. In my context, people who have the authority to ask sometimes ask for something that I can do, but that will take several hours to accomplish. I've asked, "I'm willing to do that, but do you know that it's a four-hour fix? If so, I'll start right now." A lot of times, they'll say, "Four hours? I thought it would take five minutes. If it's really four hours, don't do it." That question can really save some time, but approach it with the willingness of someone who wants to see lives changed, not someone who was looking forward to another episode of a TV show on Netflix.

Flex is really just about attitude. Can you make changes and not make your leaders regret asking? If you can, you might already have your heart in the place it needs to be.

Paul Alan Clifford

6. Following Well

"Good leaders are good followers." Those words struck something deep inside me. I didn't agree and didn't want to agree. There were so many things that my church was doing wrong, so many things that I could fix, but no one was listening to me. I immediately started thinking about reasons that following well was a bad idea. "What about Adolf Hitler? His people shouldn't have followed him! What about David Koresh or Jim Jones? No, following well is never a good idea!"

Right now, a lot of you are with me. The bumper sticker that says, "Question Authority," could be your life's verse. Sometimes you play devil's advocate just because everyone else seems to be agreeing. You think you play a valuable role in your church by making sure all the problems are solved and ways around possible roadblocks are mapped out before any action is taken. When too many people agree with the pastor, you start to think that something is wrong. You wonder if the pastor has "too much power" or is only surrounded by "yes men." You make sure you let everyone know everything that could go wrong with any given decision at any time.

That was me. For years, it was me. I served under the weight of continually pushing back against my leaders and telling them that I had a better idea. My ideas seemed so obvious that I didn't understand why no one was listening.

The truth is, I wasn't being helpful. When a young leader made a decision that required them to step forward despite their own doubts, I added my voice to the doubt category, making their job harder. I refused to believe that people had already brought up concerns, and had decided the right course of action. I had to stop "this," whatever "this" was. I was annoying to people around me, and my wife was tired of hearing my complaints about those in leadership at church.

That's when it all changed for me. Almost exactly a year after I heard the words, "good leaders are good followers," I returned to the place where I'd heard them for the first time, my church's leadership retreat. I put aside the list of "I'll never do that's" which had been accumulating for years. This wasn't a list of bad things, but a list of good ones. I'd decided that if I felt Jesus was telling me to do it, I could trust Him.

I used to think, "I'll never follow my direct leaders well and even if I start, I'll never apologize to them for how I followed poorly." Fresh after an hour of prayer, I did both of those things. I'm pretty sure the two people that I needed to apologize to didn't feel like it was the huge thing it was to me. I said, "I haven't been following you two very well. That needs to stop. I'll be better at it from now on." They thanked me. It was over very quickly.

I felt refreshed. I decided that I wasn't going to make things harder for them than I had to. To give teeth to it, I decided that I wasn't going to interject my opinion for a year. I was just going to do whateverI was told to do and not question it.

I realized that Adolf Hitler died decades before I was born. So did Jim Jones. David Koresh was from Texas, not Kentucky, where I lived. My leaders were good people who didn't make evil decisions. They sometimes made mistakes, but don't we all? I realized that no one had ever asked me to kill anyone or drink special Kool-aid. I was reacting harshly to "Hey Paul, could you change the font we use for worship?" or "Can you cut down the length of the video a bit?" These were not life and death decisions, just little things I could do to make it easier for my leaders to do what they needed to do.

I've continued on, doing better at following. I haven't always been perfect, but my heart is wrapped up in the idea that I can help just by supporting the mundane decisions that my leaders make.

Some people might be thinking that I've been brainwashed into being just a worker drone in the hive, ready to do the bidding of whatever master plan comes next. That's not the case. There are a few things that you should know about what following well isn't.

Following well is not:

1. Turning off your brain. God gave you a brain for a reason, and He wants you to use it. You should never let alarm bells ring if something has truly gone awry. You should "test the spirits" like it says in 1 John 4:1 and "take every thought captive" like Paul says in 2 Corinthians 10:5. This means that you don't give "I can't change the font; what if my leaders are evil?" a pass. Don't give something that's truly evil a pass either. Just make the filter less strict. You don't have to pass every request through it; if there are red flags, then talk to someone about them.

2. Withholding information for the sake of not disagreeing. If you know something isn't physically possible, but your leader wants to do it, it's not helpful to them to find out by experience what you already know. On the 1970s sitcom, *WKRP in Cincinnati*, the station manager wanted to give away turkeys for Thanksgiving by dropping them out of a helicopter. He believed that they could fly, but commercially farmed turkeys really can't. If your leader comes up with an idea like that, and you know the results will be disastrous, don't keep quiet just to keep the peace. Humbly speak up. This is a silly example, but you can imagine others. Maybe, your pastor wants to bring in a band for a concert, but their lights are more than your electrical service can handle. Say something about that earlier rather than later.

3. Taking delight in the failures of the leaders' ideas because you don't like those ideas. I think following well sometimes entails embracing a vision for things you might not have agreed with initially. Imagine that your pastor has just decided to change an event in a way you don't like. Embrace the vision of why he changed it and pray for success. Don't secretly hope for failure. Don't think, "When they see how screwed up this thing was, they'll know that I was right." Hope that you were wrong. Once the decision's been made, it's too late to be second-guessing. It's time to support it. Embrace it to the point that you cast the vision to others.

A couple of years after I started following well, I found a verse in the Bible that helped me. In Hebrews 13:17 "Obey your spiritual leaders, and do what they say. Their work is to watch over your souls, and they are accountable to God. Give them reason to do this with joy and not with sorrow. That would certainly not be for your benefit." (NLT)   That was a revelation to me. I hope you see that following well is part of what helps make a serving church possible.

7. Leading Up

When you're following well, there's a mistake you can make. It's easy to go from devil's advocate to yes man. Neither is all that helpful, but the yes man can sometimes be particularly troublesome because you're appearing to follow your leader, but you're not really being helpful by agreeing with bad ideas, too. That's better than hurting the process, like people do when they are always standing in the way of things, but it's better to help the process than to contribute nothing but never-ending agreement.

This isn't an easy process. "Leading up" is what Bill Hybels calls it in *Courageous Leadership*, but I think I can explain it here more succinctly. In my experience, leading up is giving your leaders the information they need and not being emotionally attached to the outcome.

If you're passionate about what you do and are skilled at it, that can be hard. In my area of service, I've spent literally thousands of hours learning about what I do and trying to get better at it. I've taken jobs solely for what they could add to my expertise. When someone tells me to do something that's doesn't jive with my experience, I can fight back (as I have in the past) or I can give information, but not be attached to the outcome.

The goal here should be to adequately explain, but it's possible to go too far in one direction or the other. Have you ever been around someone who over-explained an idea so much, that you went from engaged, to angered that he apparently thought you were unintelligent, to bored at the intricate details that no one needed to know to get the job done? That's actually something that I struggle with. I want to be understood so badly that I sometimes over-explain.

In talking with others, I've found it's much more helpful to under-explain and ask for questions, instead of giving people the false impression that you believe they're not as intelligent as you actually think they are. Try to think of the fastest way to say something before you speak. Don't use two sentences when one will do. Don't outline the background of something when they only need to know that it is a certain way today. If they ask for more, fine. If they don't, you've saved them a lot of time.

If you trust your leaders to ask necessary questions, this will help you answer the right ones. Be in conversation, not lecture mode. Trust them with how they process the information and how they deal with it too. When it has to be "my way," I'm saying that God can't use the other way or that I'm smarter than the people making the decisions.

There's nothing wrong with asking again if a question hasn't been settled. I know that I forget stuff I'm supposed to do all the time. If you don't hear an answer to a question, it doesn't mean that the answer is "no," but that the question hasn't been settled or you just haven't been told. If it has been settled, move on. It doesn't do any good to go around stewing because no one took your advice. Work on what you can work on.

Remember that strong feelings don't mean that the person having them is right. "I feel strongly that..." is a pretty useless phrase. A lot of people with strong feelings have been both certain and wrong in the past. The guy that felt strongly that the earth was flat is no more right because of his feelings than the guy who kind of thought it might be flat. Strong feelings don't tip the scale even a little bit.

I think that if you're at the table and people are asking you questions, it's wrong to keep silent, unless you don't have anything to add. If you do, submit your information, holding the results loosely. You're part of a team, so treat information like it's the ball at a pick-up game. It's no fun if one kid "hogs" it and refuses to share. That's not the way to react.

Instead, I think about a couple of friends of mine. They have every right to hoard what they have and make a little kingdom for themselves, but they don't. I don't know how much he makes, but I'm sure it's about twenty times what I make. Their home is always open to people and they are marked by their generosity. One winter, we had a major electrical problem at our house that made it unlivable for a couple of weeks. They invited my family over when they heard and we stayed as their guests for that time. I felt like a member of the family. They didn't ask anything in return. That's the way to be with your ideas and information. Share without expecting anything but the satisfaction of knowing you didn't keep necessary information to yourself.

Learn to discern the truly important from stuff you think is important. I think of it like triage in an emergency room. Some stuff must be dealt with now. Some can wait until later. Some doesn't need to be dealt with at all. Be honest with yourself about what you bring up. Timing really matters. It's not worth interrupting the pastor right before a message to talk about paint colors for the nursery, but it would be very important to let someone know before they go to pick it up that there's been a run on baby blue, so only yellow is left.

Just because it's not the right time, doesn't mean there's no right time. Moses tried to fix the condition of oppression that God's people were laboring under long before he succeeded. David was anointed king long before Saul was dead. Isaiah foretold about the Messiah's coming long before Jesus was born in Bethlehem. Sometimes people know what God's up to before it's time. It's easy to get impatient, but patience is God's way. Lead up to your leaders, but don't expect that any vision He's given you for the future will necessarily happen tomorrow. The time has to be just right.

If you're a leader, don't immediately dismiss it when someone is humbly leading up. What if Peter had discouraged Paul? What if Elijah told Elisha that he was asking for too much when he asked for a double portion of the Lord's blessing? The same Spirit is at work in the lives of your people. He might be telling them something you need to know.

Leading up is about being a part of a team and being a leader who can hear council from others. For those others, it's about not holding back what needs to be said, but sharing important information. This isn't anyone's ministry except the Lord's. We need to all remember that in our interactions with each other. We're all on the same team, trying to see lives and eternities change; let's act like it.

8. Paid or Unpaid

This question has been bugging me for quite some time. Why is the church so dependent on volunteers, when both Jesus (in Luke 10:7) and the Apostle Paul (in 1 Timothy 5:18) said, "the worker is worth his wages." They were both talking about people working to spread the gospel. Paul is clearly talking about the people in charge of the church, but Jesus isn't. He's talking to people who are basically what we'd call missionaries. They're both referring to the principle from Deuteronomy 25:4, which says that you shouldn't muzzle an ox while it's treading grain. In other words, if you help make something, you should be allowed to gain from it. An ox helps to make the grain edible, so it should benefit.

It's easy to say, "that's just one of those Old Testament rules," but Jesus and Paul both seemed to treat it with more seriousness. There are tons of rules that neither talked about. Why this one? I think it's about heart and intention.

People that volunteer have a choice to make. Are they going to support themselves with a job, like Paul did, or are they going to be in the ministry professionally? Paul talked about this very thing in 1 Corinthians 9: he said it was his right to be paid, but he chose not to be. I think that's the crux of the matter. In effect, volunteers are giving 100% of their potential salary back to the church to support its ministry. Those of us who don't get paid are taking time that we could give to our families and sacrificing it to God.

I recognize that most churches don't have the money to offer to pay their volunteers. Some might take the money if it was offered. Why is this the case?

According to the U. S. Department of Health and Human Services (http://aspe.hhs.gov/poverty/12poverty.shtml), the poverty threshold for a family of four in 2012 is $23,050. Now assume you had a church of 400 people. All equally divide into families of four, so 100 families each making exactly $23,050. That's $2,305,000. If each gave exactly 10%, the church's income would be $230,500 per year.

According to an article I read about church staffing (http://samrainer.wordpress.com/2010/04/15/lean-church-staff/), a lean church staff should have about one person on staff for each 86 people in attendance. Now, if we multiply the 4.65 staff this hypothetical church should have by $23,050 (because we're going to pay staff members what the congregation makes), we get $107,182.50, leaving $123,317.50. Depending on the building and some other intangibles, you very well might have plenty to pay for more staff (at least one or two).

A lot of the costs in running the building are fixed and don't change with more people. So for every twelve new families, assuming the building is already big enough, you could add a staff member if they all tithed.

That's the point. They all have to tithe. If you're a volunteer that wouldn't impose on your church to hire you, but spend a lot of time every week doing what needs to be done to keep the church running, but you don't tithe, you're part of the reason the church can't offer to pay you to do what you do.

I really think this matters. If you want to be a part of the church staff and volunteer 20+ hours a week to make ministry happen, you need to lead out by being a tither as well. If your leadership spawns more tithers, you might just get your wish. It also helps you to be the kind of person that God can use in ministry, a generous person.

I want to be marked by generosity. My goal is to one day give away 90% of what I make. Right now, that's impossible, but being someone who tithes regularly helps me step forward in that goal. I got this idea from Rick Warren (http://www.ted.com/talks/rick_warren_on_a_life_of_purpose.html), who is both a 90% tither and unpaid by his church. Since the royalties from his book *Purpose Driven Life* pay his living expenses, he doesn't need or want a paycheck.

Not everyone can be like Warren and give their life away for free, but I love the heart behind it. That's the heart of a serving church, not looking for gain, not asserting rights, but thinking about others first.

Church leaders are probably clapping now because of what I said about tithing. I really don't think churches should have to worry about paying to keep the lights on or have to stress about hiring the next staff member. It should be easy to pay for the next salary.

When should a volunteer become a staff member? I think that depends if someone is doing good work, and doing a lot of it. If they lost their job and had to take another out of state, where you'd lose them, and could only replace them by a paid staff member, why not prevent the potential problem by hiring them before they lose their job?

There are people that you know make the church run. They do things for free that you know would cost a lot of money if you paid them. Pray about giving them the opportunity to use the "best hours of their day" to do what they do for free now. Who immediately springs to mind as someone that needs to come on staff? Start the prayer process. If God desires it, He'll bring the money.

What about a staff position you think you need to hire, but someone is doing part of that work already? Should you hire them or look outside the church? That's a tough call. If you hire someone to do what another person is doing for free, the volunteer might not feel needed. He or she might feel like their work wasn't good enough. If that's true, talk to them and see if they have hidden abilities to take it up to the next level, or if they're just barely making it now. If you have a high capacity volunteer that would like to be on staff, but while at church she's a treasurer, but she a surgeon during the week, she might not want to take a pay cut. She might also feel called to be a big giver in your church, and a staff position means she'd neither continue in medicine nor continue to give at a high level.

Don't hire someone to replace a key volunteer without honoring his service including that him in the process. He probably knows the right questions to ask that you don't. He can probably help you weed out unqualified applicants with ease because of his expertise.

Remember that someone from the outside will take a while to assimilate into your church's culture. They won't know the ins and outs of accomplishing things that a 5-year volunteer already knows. It's possible to get an expert from the outside who is so assured of his or her expertise that he or she will be difficult to lead. The person from across the country who's been doing this for years at various churches might not be the perfect fit that a committed volunteer would be. Keep that in mind.

There are no easy answers for who should be paid and who shouldn't be. I don't think that you can just say, "They should be content to volunteer" if they're struggling to pay their bills. The same is true for a potential staff member; you can't just say, "he should be on staff" if he's good at what he does, but is a horrible fit with people. It's more complex than it seems, but my advice to volunteers is to be the best you can at what you do. To ministry leaders, my advice is to look for people that God has His hand on for the ministry. The church needs the right people, not people who just do tasks or people who are willing to move for money. That's the tricky part.

9. Getting Past the Hard

Some things are just hard. If you came to know Jesus in the hopes that your life would be a breeze, I've got bad news for you. Life can throw all sorts of things at you that you don't want and didn't expect. I'm sorry if this is news to you, but I have a feeling that it's not.

Today has been one of those days. I'm at a low spot in the income of my business and my wife's paychecks have been very helpful in keeping us afloat. She planned for a lower than normal check, but it was about 20% lower than planned. In addition, our electric bill was higher than planned. We got into a fight about money (we're not perfect by any stretch of the imagination). Then, today I got a call while I was helping to set up our stage at church that "the radiator hose on [her] car exploded." It's been a hard day.

This just happens to be one of the two biggest weekends at my church. I've noticed a pattern. Bad things happen around Easter and Fall Kick-Off when we have more than normal numbers at church.

Life is hard. Telling that to someone one who has just found out they have cancer, or saying it when a loved one dies, doesn't help at all. This reminds me of the scene in *Bruce Almighty* when Bruce is cursing God for his life and Bruce's girlfriend says, "You know everything happens for a reason." Bruce responds that that's a cliché and that it doesn't help. It's true. You can't help someone in a hard time by giving them "bumper sticker" answers. Please don't reduce the Faith to "it's God's will." Even if it is true (and in some circumstances we can debate whether God allowing something is His perfect plan), it doesn't help the person suffering.

So, back to today. Why am I writing with a sense of happiness and contentedness, given the hard things that happened? There are a couple of reasons. I have a different perspective and I know at least part of the outcome. I trust Jesus in the hard times. I've given Him permission to wreck and rebuild me into who He envisions. I fight Him a lot of the time, but at my core, I want Him to be in charge and do whatever He wants.

I know that my day was no kind of suffering. It just wasn't. I know I have brothers and sisters in far-off lands that are being tortured, imprisoned, and killed for Jesus. I always try to remember that when I have a flat or I feel like I'm near financial ruin. This isn't suffering. I echo what the Apostle Paul said in 2 Corinthians 4:17 when I say that these troubles are "light and momentary." He lived a **much** harder life than I ever have. My troubles really are light and momentary in that perspective.

I arrived at the parking lot where my wife's car was parked and found that she didn't have a broken radiator hose, just a hose that came off the place where it connected to the radiator. I was able to put it back on in thirty seconds. Once I replaced the fluids, her car was just as it was this morning.

I was told after I agreed to set up for the concert, thinking it was a volunteer gig, that I would be paid. I had a meeting today where a client told me he'd have a check for me soon. These two things will likely combine to make up the deficit from my wife's check. In addition, I have a client scheduled for Monday and Tuesday (and maybe Wednesday too). That helps a lot.

I mentioned the timing. I don't believe this is bad luck or bad karma. I think this is a deliberate act of sabotage by God's enemy, the Devil. He's shown his hand (to borrow a card term). Year after year, bad things happen around, but not often on, big days at my church. One year I came out after staying too late preparing for the next day and found my tire flat. I had to laugh. If you're a Lutheran, I hope you'll see my utter contempt of this scheme and laughter at it as something similar to Martin Luther's advice to ridicule the Devil. It really felt like a "master plan," by the understudy to a James Bond villain-in-training, to me.

These hard things drive me to prayer, you see. My first thought when my wife called was a prayer. "Jesus, I pray you'd make this repair simple and requiring no parts." I'm not the best mechanic in the world, so I had little hope if it was a complex repair that would require tons of troubleshooting. Still Jesus answered my prayer. It was easy. It was such an easy fix, my wife could have almost (almost because she's even less mechanical than am I) fixed it herself.

I think you can best help people who are struggling in hard situations by giving them perspective, trust, and knowledge of enemy plans *before* bad things happen. I didn't come to these ideas quickly or easily. I've been following Jesus for nearly thirty years now. I don't do it perfectly and I hope you'll take these ideas as strategies, not perfect answers for all situations, but they work for me. I wrote this chapter because I want to help you in the good times decide to trust in the hard times.

This chapter belongs in this book because if you serve Jesus and the Church, you're likely to run into against hard things while serving. Someone you pour yourself into will betray you. Your closest friends will abandon you. You'll feel all alone. That should sound familiar because that's what happened to Jesus. Don't see hard things as punishment for your sin. There will be some natural consequences from your sin, but sometimes bad things happen. They just do. Remember that Jesus understands. He does. For me that's the final and ultimate strategy. If you trust Him no matter what, if you expect that He'll use even evil (not just hard, but pure evil), turning it to good), it's much easier to get past.

I think that's the little secret of it all. God is powerful enough to use it all for good. At my church, during one series we smashed plates and later turned them into a mosaic, which was more beautiful than the original plates. That's what Jesus does. We smash the plates and He turns the shards into something more beautiful than the original. Trust Him to do it. It will be worth it, even when it's hard.

10. When More is Less

There are a lot of things that I call "counterintuitives." These are things that you'd think are one way, but in fact they're the opposite. Here are a few.

- In the moment, yelling feels like the most rational thing you can do sometimes, but it rarely accomplishes what you want it to.

- If you want the solution to a problem, a lot of times you need to look in the exceptions, not in the way things normally are.

- The more you serve, the less it feels like you are.

This chapter is about the last of these. It might not be that way for everyone, but for me it is. I don't get burned out when I serve long and hard, but I am likely to feel overworked if I *do* take time out.

I've been the primary video guy at our satellite campus for nearly three years. In the last eighteen months or so, we had a sound guy who, like me, is a utility player, capable of doing a good many of the tech disciplines. As a gift to me, he offered to take one Sunday a month from me. I embraced the opportunity because I hadn't had a lot of time off.

Each time my turn to have a week off came up, I noticed something about myself. I treasured it so much that I began to hate the thought of being on the next week. I don't currently feel that way, but I was seeing it and not liking it. I started to think of all the things I could do with that time, how nice it would be not to wake up at 5:50 AM every Sunday, etc. I was walking down the path of selfishness and I don't like it when that happens. Eventually, this guy's wife had a baby so he went back to the main campus, which is much closer to his house. This meant I wasn't getting regular time off, which was fine.

Earlier, I mentioned that I ran the switcher for every service at our church for eighteen months. I felt the same way. I didn't notice the time because it was just the way it was. I was tired, but since I knew why I did it, I was fine with the time.   When other people started to take over, I quickly became dissatisfied with the schedule and felt under-utilized.

I've been wondering why this is so and I think I have an idea.   It's a little like how taxes come out of your paycheck and you start to not notice it.   After a while you don't notice the time you don't have.   I'm not saying that serving is like paying taxes.   It's a lot more fun and I know that what God does with my time is a better use than what Uncle Sam does with my money.

There's another piece too.   If you're doing what you're passionate about and you know why, time just flies by.   I've been amazed how I can arrive at church at 7:00 AM and leave at 2:30 PM, and feel like I was there for two hours, not 7.5.   I don't clock watch or hope it will all end.   When I'm at church serving, I feel like I'm who I was meant to be, doing what I was meant to do.   Before I started my own ministry, I was amazed at how slowly the same seven or more hours would pass at work. Time off when I did tech support was a welcome respite from the toil of answering the same questions, from the same people, about the same products, day in and day out.

It's different at church than it is when you're doing what needs to be done to pay the bills. Work is a gift to us all that keeps us from idly frittering away our lives and accomplishing nothing, but serving is a higher level. When you're serving, you get to put aside yourself and think about others. When you're doing what you're made to do, this is fulfilling on a level that few other things are.

When you have a big enough "why" behind serving and you put your preferences aside, serving more is easy. More really is less — less stressful, less difficult, and less of a burden.

Church leaders, I really want to challenge you not to feel guilty about calling people up to a challenge. There are probably a lot of people in your church who will flourish when they serve. I don't mean you should ask them to serve once a quarter. There are people who actually need to dive in head first into the waters of life-changing service.

At my church, our pastor sometimes says, "Don't say someone's 'no' for them." If you don't have the people you need, pray for them to come and then invite them in big. The more involved you are, the better it is for your heart.

Remember that Jesus took the disciples away for three years. I bet that time flew by. Imagine it: You wake up and walk with Jesus, who shares all sorts of deep, but loving things during the journey. Someone stops your group and Jesus heals her. You stop by a house and a little girl who people were mourning for comes back to life. I can't imagine the feeling you'd get from being in on the beginning of a movement like that.

Think of the stories Peter told his wife when he'd visit home. When James and John saw their dad, what did they say? I bet they loved seeing family, but were excited to get back to a life that mattered in ways they'd only dreamt about before. Imagine it. They went from the lowest professions (either by status or popularity) to literally walking with Jesus, the Son of God. It must have been something unexplainable.

I think I know a little of how they felt. It was hard, but being constantly in the stream of God's will can be so refreshing. Have you ever wondered why Jesus said, "My yoke is easy and My burden is light" in Matthew 11:30? It's my experience that doing more for Jesus out of the overflow of your relationship with Him is easier than resisting to avoid serving.

I believe we were all made for a reason. The service you were made to do is a good portion of that reason. That's part of why serving with abandon is so much easier than putting strict limits on what you'll allow God to do with your life. Doing the latter isn't what you were made to do. It's like retrofitting a boat to drive on land. It can be done, but it won't work as well as when a boat runs on the water.

You hear people convinced that God's plan is to send them to Africa, something they're ill-suited to do. I believe that while there are those who are called to that life, they're created for it. Most of the rest of us are called to more mundane things. I say "mundane," but I don't think anything service do for Jesus is mundane, really. It's all part of a plan so grandiose that we can't wrap our minds around it, a plan that we each fit into perfectly like a puzzle piece fits exactly into its place in the puzzle. Doing what you're made to do is both giving up your life and gaining it. You're giving up your plans and preferences, and finding that what God had for you was always better. The more and more you embrace that life, the less you struggle to go down roads you don't really want to. More lives and eternities are saved when you concentrate less on yourself. More really is less.

11. Don't Do it Alone

I used to think that anything worth doing was worth doing alone. I'd been hurt by quite a lot of people in my life. I don't mean that I was beaten and left for dead. I wasn't. I was abandoned by friends and forgotten by people that I spent hours with every week. I was even abused by someone I considered my best friend.

The reason I can be so solitary is because these experiences shaped me. I just assumed that I'd always be someone who just keeps to himself. The thing is that I really like people.

When I arrived at my church with my freshly minted (and self-proclaimed) expert status in tow, I was amazed how many things were done in groups. My first experience was changing a set. I arrived because I like to help. I was surprised to find a large group of people pitching in to do a job that a couple could have done.

The thing that I came to understand, and soon appreciate for myself, was that they really liked each other. This was the early days at my church, so those of us who knew Christ felt the need to help out more; we didn't expect that those who didn't would. If it needed to be done, someone needed to do it, and it was often me.

That's not to say that there weren't others around. There were. I was rarely alone in any endeavor. I believed that I was necessary and so I was around to help.

I noticed some other things, too. Our work as a team yielded better results than my work as an individual. Someone would say, "Hey, can we…" and we did, and it looked better than what I'd envisioned. I really started to believe that teams are a better way to accomplish Kingdom work.

That's not to say that sometimes a team isn't required. Writing, for example, can be quite a solitary pursuit. Video editing can be that way, but it need not be. Sometimes a group of people to bounce things off of really helps.

I do know that a lot of people choose being alone instead of actively choosing community. While sometimes those moments are necessary and good, they shouldn't be the rule.

Our prayer team sometimes splits off to pray alone to cover "more ground," but then will come back together to agree in prayer over the things they'd each just prayed for alone.

People often mistake the meaning of the word "church" for "church building." There really is no church without the people. This is another one of those words that doesn't really mean anything to us now, but it was full of meaning at one time. Think of it as group, assembly, gathering, or community. My own church uses "community" as the middle word in our name. It's actually redundant, though. A church is a community. The word has come to mean a religious group, but it didn't always mean that. It was much more generic.

Ekklesia, the word in the New Testament that we translate as church, was almost translated by the translators of the King James Bible as "congress" instead. Now, a lot of us think of congress as a political body that is always disagreeing with one another. I think of it more as a group or exchange.

A church is a group, so the smaller activities within that church should, as often as seems wise, be done as a group. There are exceptions, so please don't think that I'm suggesting group restroom trips or anything similarly inappropriate. I am suggesting that if you do your ministry alone (with few exceptions), you're missing out on a lot of opportunities for learning and growth.

I really think this is what the author of Hebrews meant in 10:25 by "Let us not give up meeting together, as some are in the habit of doing, but let us encourage one another…" When you have a team, you can encourage each other and sharpen each other to become better.

Let's take what I do in my church as an example. It takes quite a group of people to make each weekend service. No single person can do every job. Some of our musicians play multiple instruments, but they can't run tech. Some of the tech people are cross-trained, but they can't produce. Producers lead us well, but they're not teaching pastors. Our pastors are great teachers, but they can't edit video. I can edit video, but there are a lot of things I can't do. We need each other.

Let's look at the example of a sports team. If a basketball team has one outstanding player, they might do okay. If they have a group of fairly good players that seem to know what each other is thinking, they'll be unstoppable.

A great team loves each other. A great team calls each other up to more. A great team communicates in ways that are deeper than those who are outside the team do. A great team watches out for each other. A great team seems better than the sum of their parts.

Look at the language that Paul used for the church. He didn't call her an organization, but a body. Each has a part and each is necessary. I tell people in groups at church all the time, "We need you here" or "We're better when you're with us." I really believe it.

Don't believe the lie that your team doesn't need you. They do. Don't believe that you don't need them. You do.

Leaders, encourage people to work together. You need to discourage hermits and encourage teams. Make it a cultural expectation that things are better together. I once had a leader say, "Alone bad. Together good." It's simple, but it's true.

Even if what you do at church can easily be done alone, recruit someone to at least learn it and maybe permanently join you in it. I think it's bad stewardship for any piece of knowledge to be held by only one person. Imagine all the things that can go wrong in that situation.

When my eldest was two, she broke her arm on a Saturday night before Sunday morning church. If I hadn't had another person on the team who could have taken over for me, what would I have done? When my wife had our second child, someone stepped up to give me the one week off I had during the eighteen-month run of being on the switcher. I'm glad someone was somewhat trained, but I should have done better. I should have included more people. I should have had a team at my side.

Don't make that mistake. You will be better for having a team. Trust me on that. Don't do it alone.

12. Getting Help

If you buy what I've said about needing community, you now have a new problem. How do you get people to help you? I get it. That's a hard one. I've been both great and lousy at recruiting. Let me help you with what has worked for me and what hasn't, and we'll get you a team.

Culture. Culture matters a lot. If you're at a church with a "let the pastor do it; he's getting paid" mentality, your efforts to recruit a team will be difficult. People that used to be a part of things might be hesitant to join a team if the team's past leader wasn't cared for or something else went wrong.

I once worked for a church where there was a culture of "it's not that important if I show up." Over and over again, I'd schedule meetings and make every effort to get people there, but it rarely happened. That was a cultural problem that I had difficultly overcoming. I could have done more, but I was young and insecure, so I didn't know to follow up and get people to meetings.

Recruit who you know. After six or seven years at my current church, I got to lead video for our annual outdoor music festival. I just had a problem. Everyone qualified to help was otherwise occupied. I decided to start with the hardest to fill positions and work from there. I called in every favor I had and got the morning director for one of our local television stations, a former video person who'd moved away, and a friend in town who was at another church. That solved the problem of the director positions, but not camera people. So, I just started talking about it every time I could. If anyone mentioned the festival, even in passing, I'd say something like, "and video really needs people." Slowly but surely, I recruited nine people (three shifts of three). I had to do some training, but that wasn't a bad thing.

Compare that to my time in my role at our satellite campus. My heart was to be totally committed there from the beginning, but my wife and kids weren't there with me, so it got harder and harder to stay and put the time in. I had my ears open, but I didn't really know the people there well enough to bring it up in conversation like I did earlier. Knowing people matters in recruiting.

Be shameless in recruiting. We're all busy. That's true. I still like to believe that someone will come alive when they serve in the right area. I've seen it too often to not believe it. Those who do find their calling give you reason to be shameless in calling new people in.

When I was recruiting camera people, I went in with the very real feeling that I get to do the most fun thing at church. I wasn't faking it. I believe it. I think that sort of feeling is contagious. I bet if I met you, I could make you want to take a look at video at my church as a serving team, even if every computer you touch seems to crash and you've never learned how focus works on a camera. I just think it's cool that we get to play with video and use computers to help people know Jesus. It just is.

Are they on the right team? We have a saying at our church, "Right people, right places, right times." What that means is that the best things happen when people aren't there just because there's a hole and they need to help somewhere, but feel like their role was designed for them. Don't go around looking for who you can pilfer from the youth minister when she's not looking, or the counting team when the leader goes to make a deposit. Do look for people who are currently helping where there is a hole, but might come to life in your ministry. Talk to the leader first and get permission and then try and find the perfect role for them. There might be crossover. A tech person in the kids' ministry could probably join the same team for the adults, but sometimes you'll have a bassist who really loves live sound, but didn't know that he's more needed in the area that he feels more called and equipped for. That's who you want.

Don't dismiss young people. I don't believe the children are our future (sorry Whitney); I believe they're our present. What would happen if you tapped talented youngsters earlier? I know they won't be perfect for every job, but fifth graders can certainly help with five-year-olds. High school juniors might be great at making coffee. Middle schoolers might be great at holding cables so that your camera person doesn't trip on them. People rise to our expectations. Find what a teen is good at and give her a little bit more. I bet she'll grow into it and be really happy with herself for doing it.

Offer a class in your area. If the children's ministry offered a class in babysitting, I bet you'd have a classroom filled with childless people (either young or inexperienced) who like kids. If you offer a class on getting the most out of a camera, you have prospective recruits for photo and video. If you offer a class on making a great latte, the cafe team might just find passionate baristas in the making. For those that aren't, that's fine, too. You've helped them with a skill, but it's fun to bring people who've wanted to know how to do something out of the woodwork and onto your list of interested parties.

Have a ministry fair. This is more of a church-wide thing, but if after church you have tables set up where people can meet team leaders, ask questions, and sign up for more information, you'll be surprised how many people were just looking for an easy way to connect. If you remove the friction from getting on a team, and thus make it really easy to do, a lot of people will. Just cast the vision for how great your team is, tell them that it matters, and don't soft pitch it. Give them the straight answer for why it matters, even when it's hard.

Above all, pray. If God wants it to be done, He can bring people to help you do it. Why not ask? I'm amazed at how, after walking with Him for around 30 years, this so often slips my mind. I think it's great to get down on your knees, clasp your hands and...scream to heaven for help like your life depends on it! Don't give up with one prayer; beg until you get an answer. You can't change a heart or mind, but God can. Ask Him to do just that. When I was in seminary, our president used to say, "What if there are some things that God can't do or God won't do, until and unless His people pray?" I don't think he meant that God is unable to do some things, but that His nature requires Him to wait until someone asks for help in some areas. What if one of those areas is bringing help? Isn't that what Jesus meant when He said to "Ask the

Lord of the harvest, therefore, to send out workers into his harvest field," in Matthew 9:38? I think it was. Prayer should be foundational to all we do. So let's pray, and I think you'll see prayers answered; you'll get some help.

13. Expect Resistance

Some time in college I started to think the devil was metaphorical, that there was no literal Satan, but that we were our own worst enemies. I don't believe that anymore. To borrow a card term, I fell for the bluff until he showed his hand. Too often, I've seen bad things happen at certain times. I can predict when they're coming. Now, I'm not surprised. I know that Jesus wasn't speaking metaphorically, and neither were the other authors of the Old or New Testament. There is an enemy and he hates us. The more ground you're taking from him for the Kingdom, the more he hates you. He has a problem though. There are too many churches and too many people who are doing God's work to oppose them all. He's under-resourced for his mission.

In the beginning of the Church, he and his forces could oppose nearly everything that the Apostles and early churches did. Now, it's more difficult. Sure, there are churches that aren't really doing anything worth opposing, but there are tons of others, all over the world, which are.

I've noticed that he'll try to do things to automate the process whenever possible. It makes sense. If your job is to keep people from doing what God has for them, starting a fight or distracting people in other ways is a great way to do it. Sadly, it's simple to veer away from doing God's will and into doing things that seem good, but are distractions from your calling. I've done it plenty, so don't feel like I'm thinking of you; I'm thinking of me and I assume that a lot of people are like me.

Earlier, I told you about some of the resistance I faced on a particular day. A couple of days after that, we had all manner of problems. The audio for the video recording was missing. The backup recording was also missing. I spent an extra hour or so aligning it. It turned out that an audio patch bay had dust built up in the very four connections we needed. The next day, the video was out of sync even though it was great the night before. One of the other guys overslept. There was a problem with starting the video on time. Lyrics were forgotten. In short, it was a bad day. Why? Coincidentally (or not), it was also one of our two largest services of the year.

Expect opposition. It really exists. If things are always easy, something is wrong. You're not a big enough target yet. Since you expect it, let's take a look at the forms it takes. I'm not saying that everything that's difficult that happens is "an attack from the devil," but that suspicious timing is often a dead giveaway.

1. Relational challenges. Suppose everything has been going great with your spouse, children, friends, and leaders, but suddenly an issue long dealt with resurfaces. You say something in jest and another person hears it as hurtful. You find yourself feeling on edge when you're normally easy going. These are all indications that something is wrong.

Sometimes when my wife and I argue, we realize it's all a big misunderstanding. During the moment, it feels like she's saying hurtful things that she'd never say. I say it's like a mean translator is standing between us. I say something innocuous, but she hears something mean-spirited and offensive. Later, when emotions cool, we realize that each was not trying to hurt the other; it just felt like that. That is what these relational challenges often feel like.

If you want to beat this challenge, the best way is to be humble and admit wrong as often as you can. Maybe something was triggered by an instance that wasn't your fault, but you can still apologize for your part in it. Assume that you had a part to play, figure out that part, and make it right.

2. Technical Challenges. I've had a flat tire, missing audio, a bad video recording, a bad hard drive, crashing worship software, a power surge, and a video switcher that only rebooted itself during the message.

One of our elders once told me, "It seems like the enemy likes to attack electronics." I know that's not in the Bible, but it sure seems like my experience. I wonder if stringed instruments would break strings or oil lamps quit working in biblical times. I think they might have.

3. Financial challenges. Haven't bounced a check since college? Are all your bills paid up? Your car just happens to break down. Your water bill is so high that you know you must have a leak. The roof in your garage starts leaking right over your lawn mower. These things happen every day. That's life. When they happen in combination at a time when God is really working, and they try to interfere with your service, that should raise eyebrows.

What to do. Remember what Paul says in Romans 8:37, "...we're more than conquerors." Be prepared for what will happen. I start praying any time I get the feeling that something bad might happen. At worst, I get to spend time with Jesus. At best, He prevents some of the enemy's schemes. It's a win-win. Prayer is your first line of defense.

In the past, I've had someone recruited to pray for me. For years it was my buddy Ben. It's been a number of different people, but lately I've been lax. I really need to get someone to do this for me, to lift up my arms like Joshua did for Moses.

There are other practical and more tangible things you can do too. You can have backups in place. Keep everything well-maintained. Do a preliminary check to make sure everything is as it should be, when you still have plenty of time and opportunity to fix it.

You should also study up on spiritual warfare. That's not my area of expertise, but people like Neal T. Anderson are great resources. Ask around for people who can help you.

Share the load as well. Remember what I said earlier about community? That really matters when you're facing opposition to the work you're doing.

Look at the Book of Acts and Paul's letters for how to react. I won't be exhaustive in what I say, but Paul said that our enemies aren't people, but powers and authorities in the unseen realms. He talked about our struggles being light and momentary. Peter said that the devil is like a lion looking for someone to devour. That's all true.

Just remember that we know the end of the story. God wins. Someday, I'm convinced, we'll look back at the stuff we faced and laugh at how trivial it all seems. Then, it will be so easy to trust God, but now we're only seeing part of the picture. Can we expect resistance? Oh, yeah. Will it cause the message of Christ to die out? No way! It's just gnats attacking an army. The victory is sure because of Who is calling us onward.

14. Eating an Elephant

In everyone's mind is a to-do list. I know there is in mine. This list has all the aspirations that you have. It's things like writing the great American novel, becoming a better spouse, learning HTML, or taking a trip around the world. This list occupies us in the quiet times. I think it lives in a place inside our psyches that refused to let go of these ideas.

For me, that list used to have my first book, *Podcasting Church*. I wrote it in 2010, but that's not when I had the idea. I had the idea in 2007. I just didn't know if I could do it. Writing a book seemed like such a huge and daunting task that I didn't think I could ever do it.

Two things combined to change my perspective. First, I heard an advertising podcast called The Monday Morning Memo (http://www.mondaymorningmemo.com/). I don't recall why I started listening, but I'm glad I did. Roy Williams, the host, talked about people in my exact situation. They kept meaning to do things. They just never did.

About this same time, I heard about NaNoWriMo. The challenge is to write a novel (or in my case nonfiction) in a single month. I decided to try. It didn't seem too hard to write 1,200 or so words a day. Forty days later, I had a rough draft.

There's an old saying, "How do you eat an elephant? One bite at a time." Anything that's difficult can be done if you just break it up into small enough pieces and "eat" them one at a time. Want to learn a new skill? Do it in small bursts.

This is just part of the equation, though. Doing something in small pieces is destined to fail if you just plan to do it when you get time or when you get inspired.

A lot of good intentions never pan out. I've said over and over, "I'll do that tomorrow." Time after time, tomorrow never came. I meant to do it, but I didn't.

The other piece of the puzzle is simple. Just do it every day. When you wake up, do you think about when you'll brush your teeth? Do you think, "Hmm, when will I eat lunch? I might be able to wedge it in." No, these are things that you do every day around the same time.

What's really worked for me is Jerry Seinfeld's productivity secret (http://lifehacker.com/281626/jerry-seinfelds-productivity-secret). It really makes sense. Maybe it's my personality, maybe it's how I'm wired, but I have to make progress every day. If I skip some, one day becomes two, which then become weeks.

It doesn't matter what the project is; if you divide it into smaller "bites" and make some progress every day, eventually you'll look back at what you've done and be amazed at the progress you've made.

I don't know how old you are, but I'm 38. I just realized a few weeks ago that twenty years ago, I was just starting college. One of the things I did when I started was journaling. I didn't do it for long, but what if I had? If I'd written 500 words a day on average for 365 days a year for 20 years, I'd have written 3,650,000 words between then and now. If you were to imagine that a book is 80,000 words (a lot are shorter, like this one, and some are longer, but let's just say 80,000), that's 46.5 books worth of words. That's a lot of books. By comparison, Stephen King has written 50 (although his are often longer).

Do you get the point? When you let time be your friend, not your enemy, you can accomplish something that people didn't think was possible. The longer you do something, the bigger it will be given enough time. Each thing builds on the one before. That, over time, creates something huge.

So, if you take something big, "an elephant," carve it up into smaller "bites," "eat" some every day, and continue for a long time, you'll eventually complete the task that seemed monumental before you started.

You should know that any task like this takes self-discipline (or self-leadership if you prefer). There are times when you won't want to do it. For me, the beginning is full of hope and promise, the middle is where it gets hard, until it's over half done; then I know I can just continue and the race toward the end seems faster and faster.

Ironically, I didn't write at all yesterday. I normally have each section done by 9:00 the next day after I start it. As I'm writing, I'm already almost three hours past my self-imposed deadline. I could make excuses, but I won't. What matters is that I'm writing now. That matters to you too.

Always have a plan for when you're not perfect. I've yet to write or do anything that went exactly according to plan and kept perfectly on schedule. Today could have been a day to feel sorry for myself and put off what I'm doing over and over again until I found myself in tomorrow. Instead, recognizing that I needed to get back to it, I started writing.

Having a recovery plan is key to accomplishing anything that's big. When I first started podcasting, I recorded every Tuesday, but I had a backup plan to record on Thursdays. That worked well and carried me through the first fifty or so episodes. Don't beat yourself up for not being perfect. You aren't. That's like being mad at yourself for having brown eyes instead of blue. It's just the way it is. Accept it. Celebrate movement that goes in the right direction and recover from misses and setbacks.

I want you to apply this procedure to your serving too. It doesn't apply only to big projects like building a new building or an annual festival. This applies to your service and your life in general. Don't look at where you want to be and give up. It's something big. It takes consistent effort over time.

What if God is less impatient with your progress than you are? What if He sees events on the horizon that He'll use to transform you into the person He knows you were meant to be? Let's look at generosity. I've told you that I want to eventually give away most of what I make. How does this work when I have trouble being generous right now when times are tight? I think the small gifts when you're poor help you prepare to give larger ones when you're not.

As our church moved from our first location to the second, there was a substantial shortfall. Our pastor called the leading families together and said, "We've done everything we can do as a church to get to this point. The only way we're going to finish is if we all sacrifice to do it." My wife and I knew we should, but times were tight. How could we participate? We both felt like God was telling us not to go to the grocery store for one month (the time we had), and give that money to the church. I knew it sounded crazy, but I believe that I should do what God asks. During that time, people who didn't know what we'd done (because we didn't tell anyone) kept giving us food. One friend stopped by and said she'd cleaned out her pantry and wanted to know if we wanted what she found. My mother and sister came for a visit and brought food with them. Time after time, we were taken care of when we didn't see how we could be. When you trust God for your food, it's easier to trust for luxuries. If He loves me enough to make sure I don't go hungry, maybe I can also trust Him to make sure that I get what's best for me, and I shouldn't worry whether or not I get that vacation.

That's how this process works. Look for opportunities to grow and keep going. Sometimes it will be faster and sometimes it will be slower, but eventually, you'll look back and realize you're nearly done, and you'll wonder how it happened.

15. Playing to Your Strengths

There's a freedom that comes from knowing yourself and what you are made to do. I know a lot of what I can't do, and it frees me not to do it. I also know a lot of things that I'm okay at, but don't have the passion to pursue. There are only a few things that I'm good at, want to be better at, and have the passion to do what it takes to get that way.

When I first started going to my church, I chose not to do a lot of things that I could do in favor of what I was called and gifted to do. As a result, I've concentrated on and honed those gifts. I've always felt as though I was made to do what I was doing, so I was able to continue in hard times. This is especially true now. As I'm struggling to make this ministry self-sufficient, I get a deep feeling of satisfaction when I lay my head on the pillow at night, knowing that while I wasn't perfect in my actions, I'm now closer than I ever have been.

I think that most people's abilities are shaped not by some innate ability, but by the gift of desire that the Lord places in them. There are prodigies that can do all manner of interesting things with little or no instruction. Most of us are physically able to do any number of things well, but choose not to because of priorities.

That sounds noble, but it doesn't have to be. I chose not to train and nurture my swimming talents because I preferred to watch TV. I chose not to work on a senior honors project in Philosophy when I was in college because I preferred to spend time with my new girlfriend, who subsequently left me. We all have priorities. Sometimes we choose well and sometimes poorly.

Now I nurture my gifts, those things I feel I was created to do, because of the results I think God wants to achieve. I think this is what separates talents from gifts — their purpose. I haven't so far turned *Podcasting Church* into *Podcasting for Small Business* or *Tweeting Church* into *Twitter for Non-Profits* because I don't feel like God told me to write them so that I could make as much money as I could. I've had a couple of people tell me I should do minor rewrites so that they're more generic, but I've never been happy doing work to help companies make a buck, or to help other organizations temporarily soothe the symptoms of the diseases that the Church is called to cure.

Determining what your priorities ought to be is difficult. I could have just as easily chosen drama, music, or speaking at church, but I didn't. Why?

When I started doing video, I found within it a drive that I hadn't felt before. As a serial procrastinator, I'd put my assignments off for days, weeks, months, and in one case, a whole semester. When I took a class on technology, I found myself rushing back to my dorm to put what I'd learned into practice before I forgot it. See the difference? I'm not the best videographer in the world, but I want to learn more and more. That's the first indication that you're on the right track. If you find what you're doing to be so refueling that what others consider work, you consider play, maybe you should do more of that.

I also noticed that as I went down the path toward doing video, a word kept cropping up that I didn't think applied to me. Many in the church with this label were people I looked up to for what they did and how they did it. I never thought I could be one, but something somewhere deep inside, I always wanted to be an artist. Do you secretly wish you could be a technician, a speaker, or a helper, but right now you don't feel that you could live up to the label? Maybe that's who you are, but you just need more time and practice to meet your own standards.

What are you afraid to try because you fear that failing at it would be crushing? For me, that was writing. I so wanted to write a book, but was so sure that I'd fail that I didn't dare try. What if I tried to write a book and it was only ten pages long? What if this dream was dashed permanently? What could I cling to and wish I could do then? My experience says it's much better to make progress on your dream than to only hope that someday you will. Fear is a trick that mostly keeps each of us from doing the great things God has designed us to do. Don't give into it.

I also think that you should pursue strengths that point to Christ and not to yourself. What's the difference between an Old Testament prophet like Isaiah, who foretold things long before they happened, and a psychic that tells what will happen in the next year and prints it in a supermarket tabloid? Isaiah wasn't trying to build his kingdom, but God's. Someone who says, "I can see that such and such will happen" is different from someone who says "I get a feeling from Jesus that such and such will happen," even if their predictions were to agree. I want my gifts not to become famous, but to make Jesus famous. I want to fade into the background and have Him in the spotlight.

I've been told on more than one occasion that the lists of gifts in the New Testament are not exhaustive. Because of this, I've noticed little quirks about myself that seem to be helpful to others. I don't know if they're spiritual gifts, strictly speaking, but doing what's helpful isn't bad, so I continue on. Pay attention to anything in yourself that might seem minor, but that you do better than others. Are you the first to notice a new hairstyle? I actually am. This isn't helpful to me, but I make sure I compliment people when I notice and tip off sometimes clueless husbands to help them score brownie points with their wives. It's a bit like encouragement, but smaller and more specific. I can sense when a message point needs to be punctuated by applause and when I start, others tend to follow. It's a little like leadership, but smaller and more specific. How about you? What ancillary minor gifts can you nurture so that they help others? Do you notice punctuation mistakes in worship lyrics? Maybe you could help proofread. Do you have trouble passing up a piece of trash that others seem not to notice? You're helping make the environment inviting to newcomers when you clean it up.

We're all made differently from each other. When you discover the strengths you have and work to build them, Jesus should be built up. Lives should be altered. The Kingdom should grow. Pay attention. You're not given these gifts for yourself. Like love and forgiveness, they're meant to be shared.   It's in the sharing that you really are using your gifts as God intended, to help others.

16. Getting Better

I don't think that having a gift means that you're automatically as good as you're going to be. I think it means that you're directed by a God-given passion toward developing it. There are exceptions, but I think that the more you do anything, the better you get at it. Long processes get shortened. Ideas that you thought would work are abandoned in favor of those that do. It's something that happens over time.

Don't assume that you'll get better at your gifts by doing nothing. You need to invest in yourself. This may sound strange, but what I mean is that you need to take what God has invested in you and make it more and more useful to the Kingdom.

1. Be a self-feeder. Don't wait for someone to pick you out of the crowd and say, "Let me invest in you." Instead, look for ways to do it yourself. If you're a musician, this might be as simple as stretching your musical tastes and going to concerts. If you're a leader, find leadership blogs to read. If you're great at hospitality, find ways to do what you do more efficiently without sacrificing quality. Just do it yourself. The point here isn't that you shouldn't need others, but that you can learn and grow without asking for permission.

2. Attend conferences. I love a good conference. Whether I'm teaching or learning, there's nothing like what you get out of attending one. The first conference I ever attended with my church was the "Willow Creek Arts Conference" in 2001. I thought that I knew everything about my art until I was around the people who did it for Willow Creek. They really helped me grow into a better artist.

Conferences don't need to be huge either. I learned a lot at the "Business of Writing International Summit," which had a couple of hundred people. "Podcamp Cincinnati" was also a great time where I learned a lot. I also taught sessions at these conferences, and the questions the attendees asked stretched me and caused me to really apply my experiences.

You should note that the last two conferences that I mentioned were secular, at least nominally, and that meant that I got information that I wouldn't get at a Christian conference. Sometimes that's very helpful. Perhaps you wouldn't go to a secular healing conference (if such a thing exists at all), but pastors might benefit from a conference for professional speakers. Authors can certainly benefit from a conference for writers. A different perspective might break you of patterns that seem holy because they're what you're used to, but have no benefit other than familiarity.

3. Get a mentor. Timothy had Paul. The disciples had Jesus. Having a mentor to lead you is a great way to stretch and grow. I've actually done this on a couple of occasions and it's been valuable to me. As I was learning evangelism, a guy named Mason helped me stretch. As I learned more about video, Doug led me. Mentors help us see our blind spots and lead us to where we need to go, but wouldn't go by ourselves.

4. Join a forum or discussion group. I have life-long friendships that developed as a result of the first time I did this. There's nothing better than going to a conference and getting a hug from a guy who I don't recognize only, to realize that Phil is actually "SKStarkiller" from the online church technology forum I frequented. There are a ton of other people that I've met once or twice, but who I feel a kinship with that is unlike many others because we share a common gift. Some are friends, some are fans, some are mentors, but when you find a group like this and you really gel with them, it will change your life forever.

This kind of group doesn't have to be online. Local churches can connect with each other and form groups of similarly gifted people between them. Why shouldn't children's pastors get together at least once a month and learn what's working in other places and support each other in their common struggles? I'd love to see denominational differences put aside so that we can all grow together in our abilities, so that we can serve the Church more effectively.

5. Read books. The people you interact with don't need to be around or even alive. What I mean is that authors can teach across time and space. We know it's true of the Bible, but it's also true of people who've written things that are more contemporary. If you're a reader, spend time browsing your local bookstore or Amazon.com for material to help your gifts grow. Photographers can study the photography of Ansel Adams to see if any of his techniques can help your work in capturing the majesty of God. Those who teach classes can benefit from books about educational theory. The possibilities are endless.

6. Observe what works. Sometimes growing is just as simple as watching. Watch how another sound engineer mixes. Pay attention to how another church you visit on vacation takes up the offering. Listen to other pastors preach. I can't walk into a church with a projector without noticing how they project lyrics and what backgrounds, transitions, fonts, and colors they use. It happens so easily that I have to make sure that I don't get lost in the how and miss what the pastor is saying. Avoid that mistake, but do learn what you can, and don't be critical if you're farther down the path than they are.

7. Practice, practice, practice. The more you practice, the better you'll get. I'm told that writers get better by writing. Speakers get better by speaking. Musicians get better by playing. The more you do what you do, the better you will get.

This means you have to start, so don't put off the beginning of improvement because you're not where you want to be. Accept the fact that in six months or five years, you'll look back on what you did and think you were horrible. That means that you'll be better then, so start making your future self ashamed of your present self! It's actually a great thing. If you didn't look back at your spelling prowess from the first grade and think "How could I have ever thought 'hair' was spelled with an 'e'," that would mean that you still thought it was. Let me say it another way. If you're not amazed at how bad you were at something after a long period of practice, you haven't gotten much better. I believe that you can get better. Even the greatest among us get better, so get started.

8. Take risks. The biggest breakthroughs in your growth often happen when you do something unexpected. When you try to expand your abilities, you find you can do what you couldn't before. It was a huge risk for me to go out on my own and start doing what I do. Sometimes I've really hated the results. Most of the time, though, I wake up in the morning excited that I get to do what I know I'll eventually be good enough at to really help a lot of churches. Was I scared? Oh, yeah. Would I do it again? You better believe it. My pastor says leaders lead above their heads. That means you stretch into risky territory. So how are you risking? How are you doing things differently now than before? How are you doing something dangerous for Jesus? Let me know.

What if you look back at today as the day that it all changed? Start now! Imagine what your life will be like when you've quit making excuses and started to make progress.

17. Being a Lifer

We live in a society that is more and more mobile. It's not unusual for a person to move several times during his or her lifetime for a new and better job. What you don't see very often is people moving or refusing to move because of their church. Think about it. Why is this such a strange idea? You'd move for better schools for your kids. You'd move to a bigger house with more amenities. Why not stay where you are because you love your church, or why not move to where God is already doing more than you've seen before?

I think this sounds so strange to our ears because we view church as a commodity. Denominational labels further this misconception. It's easy to think that one Methodist church is like another and one Presbyterian church is like the rest.

In some ways, denominationalism is the same as franchising is for restaurants. Let's say you really like McDonald's. Almost anywhere in the world you go, there's a McDonald's. You'll find cheeseburgers, french fries, and milkshakes. You're not going to find pizza at most McDonald's. Likewise, if you want a high church service, you'd head to a Lutheran church. If you want contemporary music, you'd go to a church with a trendy name like "Compassion" or "Bridgepoint." If you only go to your church because of the style of worship, you can find that style almost anywhere you go, just like you can find cheeseburgers almost anywhere you go.

What if you're looking for something different, something rare? I'm not talking about a great children's program or a class in Greek. There are churches that are taking territory away from the Enemy. When people walk through the doors, they leave changed. God does the work in these churches, but there's something about the culture that facilitates His work. Maybe it's prayer, an emphasis on evangelism, or something else, but whatever it is, people who call themselves atheists attend and eventually become Christians. That's the kind of church I go to. I'm convinced that if I can get the people that I know who are far from God to hang around people from my church long enough, they'll come to know Jesus. I've seen it too often to question it. Lives and eternities change daily at my church.

Unfortunately, that's something that doesn't happen all that often at every church. I wish you could go to any city, go into any church, and know that people who used to be atheists are becoming elders. I wish you'd see addicts becoming pastors. I wish you could see people on the brink of divorce having their marriages restored and becoming leaders in helping others. Unfortunately, what's normal at my church isn't normal everywhere.

That's why people have moved to Lexington to go to my church. It's not a perfect place. Sometimes there's friction between people, but I've never been a part of a church like this before. Grace permeates everything. We all talk about how we're broken. We all realize that we need Jesus more than we need to look like we have it all together.

I've told my leaders that I'm going to this church until they carry me out in a pine box. I'm a lifer. You see, I've always wanted to be a part of a church like this. The words in Acts 2, "and the Lord added to their numbers daily, those being saved," quicken my heart. They always have. When I was young, I recall reading that line and thinking, "What would it be like to be a part of a church where people were daily coming to know Jesus?" Something in me used to mourn the fact that I was born in the twentieth century instead of the first, even though I really like computers, air conditioning, and the internet.

Once I found a place where I was helping people come to know Christ, using my gifts, and really making a difference, I was hooked. I acknowledge that my church has areas it can grow in. It's made of people, so things often happen that need to be worked through. I think all churches are like that if people are actually sharing who they are and not hiding behind perfect Sunday masks.

There are some things you can do to help your intentions to stay with a church for life. The first is to acknowledge that God has the final word. Should He decide that I need to move, I will go. So far that hasn't happened, but if it does, I'll make sure I'm hearing correctly and then I'll go.

When you're planning on being at a place for fifty or more years, you need to lay a ground work for that plan. I refuse to treat others like they're temporary additions in my life. Whether it's the pastor or someone I just met, I need to treat these people like they're going to be my friends for life. I don't agree politically with all of them. I don't agree with everyone's life choices. Some personalities are difficult. They're all people that Jesus loved enough to die for, and I have to keep that in mind.

All relationships are susceptible to the "grass is greener" syndrome. Churches are no exception. If you're myopic in what you're looking at, other places will look better. You might think, "They've got better music," or "They treat their volunteers better." That might be true, but the thing about thinking that the grass is greener is that you overlook the brown spots. That's why married people who have affairs are briefly convinced the object of their affection is perfect, even though that's far from true. If anything is perfect, your imperfection will ruin it, so don't be tempted to join it. There should always be growth areas. If you don't see them, that just means they're hidden or you're overlooking them, not that they don't exist.

In my experience, the best way to deal with people is to address problems as they arise. Don't hold onto hurts. Be restored in your relationships with the people who hurt you. I think of it this way: if you have a list of ways people have offended you, it's better to deal with that list when it's short than to deal with it when it's an insurmountable Everest-sized pile of hurt. Talk to them about it. Don't stew in your anger. Don't put off dealing with it until hate is the natural outcome.

It's also possible to become disenchanted, not with any one person, but with the church as a whole. To really become invested in the mission of the church, you have to be a part of it. While it sometimes happens that a really involved person will get angry and leave suddenly, that's the exception, not the rule. People that are involved in the ministries of a church care more about them than those that sit in the seats "being fed." There's something about service that makes it possible to be a part of a church for decades, not just weeks or months.

Look around. Are you called to be at your church for the rest of your life? Do you believe in the vision so much that you can't help but ooze it from your pores? Have you seen your life or the life of someone really close to you affected by God at your church? Are you a lifer? If so, tell you pastor or immediate leader, and serve Jesus by serving the Church in a way that the news will make your leaders happy to know you're there until you die. That's my goal.

18. Champions of Unity

Some events change your life. The two stories I'm about to tell you changed mine. While I was in seminary, I got a job at a small church ninety minutes from campus. I loved the church and the people there. My fiancée and I would have probably moved there after seminary because we were within a month of getting married, but then it happened.

I got a call from the pastor. There was talk that I'd planned to tell the youth group about sex with my soon-to-be wife. At this same time, my fiancée's grandfather was close to death. I was with her family three hours away when I got the call.

He knew it wasn't true. I told him what had happened. It was a comment in passing during a lesson I was teaching. The material said, "Sex in marriage is great," or something like that. I followed the material, but without thinking added, "I'd have to get back to you on that." One of the teens misheard that.

He didn't ask me about it. He asked an adult. The adult didn't ask me, but started spreading it around. In less than a week, the whole church was abuzz about what I'd supposedly said.

I could have gone back for the emergency meeting about me, but I chose to be with my new family through the death of the closest person I'd had to a grandfather since I was a week old. I resigned from my position. I was the victim of gossip.

A year later, my wife and I were part of another church. This time, I wasn't the victim; it was the pastor. One night after a business meeting, where one of the senior members had failed to take "her church" away from the pastor and the leaders in charge, I watched as she sat down and started yelling that she'd been pushed. No one believed her except her husband, who arrived at the pastor's house and attacked him with a cane. The pastor defended himself, and in the process the old man fell.

The police came and arrested the pastor for assault. He was hauled off to jail. The pastor was eventually acquitted, but it was too late. He'd left his job and the church had split.

What do these two circumstances have in common? Both were a result of someone not solving conflict with the other party, but bringing others into the mix.

Sin is sin. If you ask any Christian, they'll tell you that. Deep down, a lot of people think that murder is worse than gossip. On some level, it feels like there are different grades. They're all bad, but bad is relative, right?

No. "The wages of sin is death." That's not something I made up. The apostle Paul wrote it nearly 2,000 years ago in Romans 6:23. Gossip murdered my job as well as my former pastor's. These were two churches in two locations. They shared the same problem.

You're about to read some strong words from me. That's because I believe this with every ounce of my being. Jesus told us how to deal with conflict. It's very simple, and it's outlined in Matthew 18:15 and following. Don't talk it over with your spouse; don't tell someone "you're concerned" about the one who offended you. Go to them. That's it. If it doesn't work, there are other things to do, but first, go to them.

Look at what would have happened if the people in either of these situations had gone with this advice. I would have heard immediately that someone misheard me, and I could have explained that it was an off-handed comment with no intention of over-sharing. If the older lady had kept her grievances between herself and the pastor, the police wouldn't have been called in because her husband wouldn't have fallen and injured himself when he tried to confront what his wife accused the pastor of.

How well do you do this in practice? What steps should you take? I want you to be a fierce defender of unity. Division is one of the biggest things that can keep a church from reaching its potential. It's hard to feed the sick, clothe the naked, and see lives and eternities changed if you are busy listening to and repeating rumors about who did what. You don't want to be a part of a church where the things people gossip about actually happen. Here's the sad thing. Most of the time they don't happen. The accusation brings ministry to a halt and most of the time, it's false.

I think it's so sad that pastors can't be alone with a member of the opposite sex anymore. Sometimes it's not wise, but a lot of times, it's a precaution to keep gossip at bay. I think it's sad when rumors have to be addressed, when they shouldn't have started in the first place.

Start with yourself. Don't take any grievance to anyone other than the one who can do something about it: the one who sinned against you. Take this seriously. Once you tell someone else, even your spouse, the repetition of the story might give it life it didn't have before. "Pastor so and so really ought to check his Greek about the meaning of Jesus' words on the cross" can quickly become "Pastor so and so didn't graduate from seminary because of bad grades in Greek." It's not a big jump, but it can ruin careers and lives. Refuse to be the origin of any possible gossip.

Don't let your friends get away with it either. If you hear someone say, "...and then she said to me that...," stop them. I know this is hard, but think of all the people who've had to leave their churches because of this issue. Have the friend confront the person they're accusing. Go with them if you have to. Eventually, your presence will stop people from talking about people who aren't there.

If you want to take it up a level, and you have the fortitude to do it, stop any talk you hear, no matter the source. If it helps you, think of the church as Jesus' bride. Think of that person spreading lies about some other part of her body. It's a little sick when you think of it that way. Men, how would you feel if someone was saying that your wife had a disease from sleeping around as a teen, when you know neither is true? Take it that seriously.

What's the opposite of all of this? Unity. Jesus prayed for it in John 17. Why? I think he knew the challenges that would be ahead of us. Church splits are more common than they should be. We need to show our love to an unbelieving world by being unified, not fighting over some disagreement or spreading lies about one another.

I think this is one of the things that you, as a servant in your church, can start doing right now to affect the ministry for the better.

Don't beat up people who you think are spreading rumors and not dealing with the source of their anger directly, but do treat it seriously. Treat them like you'd want to be treated when you interrupt or cut off discussion, but please prevent the kind of pain that was caused by the two situations I talked about above.

What if every Christian talked about other denominations, other believers, etc., with respect and love? What if we saw our differences as minor details that don't really matter? What if the church were the place where you could go and **not** feel like you would be judged? I think those actions would convince people who think we're all hypocrites that we're not. I think we'd be known by our love, not our divisiveness.

19. Remember the Alternatives

Have you ever had a moment that could have gone another way? One road leads in one direction, and the other is the life you're living. Think of it as the road you didn't travel. What would the results have been? What if one day in your life had changed? What would your life be like now?

If we hadn't run out of garbage bags at a freshman orientation event at my college, I might not have met my wife. If I hadn't met her, a lot of the decisions I've made would have been different. I wouldn't have the two daughters I have and might not be at the church that I'm at now.

So, how about you? How could your life be different than it is? As you're serving in a hard season, can you remember the alternatives that you rejected, which brought you to where you are?

I could be working in an ill-fitting ministry right now. There were a couple of times that I could have stayed on a path toward children's ministry, youth ministry, or even church administration. I was there for a season. They're great ministries, but not for me. They weren't my calling.

Each time, something changed and guided me toward where I am. I get to do what I love to do. When I look at what my life could have been, I'm very grateful for the forks in the road that changed things.

This idea is a bit like the one Garth Brooks talked about in "Unanswered Prayers." I'm not a country music fan, but this song has a sentiment that I think we can all learn from. Sometimes what you really want isn't what you will eventually want. I can list the things I really, really wanted in the past that would have detoured me from where I am now.

This is the antidote for the grass is greener syndrome. Is life perfect for anyone? No, I don't think it is, but when you're doing what you know you were made to do, sometimes it gets hard. When I'm up late writing, I can easily think, "I wish I could just work 9:00 to 5:00 and be done," but the thing, is I remember working 9:00 to 5:00 and hating it.

When I'm at church and something has gone catastrophically wrong, it's easy to think, "I wish I was at a church where it was simple, where I was seen as a genius," but I remember being in places where there weren't challenges to overcome. My pastor says, "To wish away the hard is to wish away leadership." I agree. I don't want to wish away what I've always wanted — to have an eternal impact.

Remembering the alternatives is all about looking at the ways that God has guided you to where He wants you to be. Christians love Jeremiah 29:11, but sometimes we forget that the path to God's good plans aren't easy and filled with fame and riches. Sometimes they're really, really hard.

Think about the disciples. They literally followed Jesus. They forgot more than we know about Him. Were their lives easy? Did they wake up every day in luxurious country estates with no problems to deal with? Of course not. Most of them were martyred.

Now look at your life. Don't give into guilt or self-condemnation; that's not my point. I want you to look at your life, no matter how bad it is, and think about the ways that it could be worse. I've had a tough spot financially, but I'm still sitting in my house, watching a television, typing on a laptop computer. That's really not that bad of a life.

I love my wife. We don't have a perfect relationship at all times, but I wouldn't go back in time and change my decision to be with her. My kids aren't perfect, but I wouldn't change the decision to have them.

I want you to approach your service the same way. Look for things to be thankful for. One at a time, name those things that you're thankful for. Think about the old hymn "Count Your Blessings" and heed its advice.

I was setting up at our church for a concert by a Christian band you've probably heard of, and I had to go. I came back and continued to help. The technical director at our church said to those of us who were still there, "Guys, thanks for staying; it really helps." I responded, "Robbie, this is no kind of suffering. We get to move cool tech equipment around to help change lives and eternities." That's the attitude you can have, a "I'm not suffering; I'm having a great time" kind of attitude.

This is all possible because I really, really trust that I'm living the life that God has designed for me, and I'm loving it. If you don't believe that you're living that life, ask yourself why. Are you on your way, but you're not there yet? Be patient. If you're stuck or if you're going the opposite direction, what life are you waiting for?

The life that God has for you is so much better than any you could design for yourself. He has the power to change things you can't. He loves you more than you love yourself. He can see what you can't see. Trust Him.

Do you have a list of things you think you should be doing to be living the life God has for you? Take one small step toward doing something on that list. I'm not telling you this because I haven't had a list myself, but because I have. I wanted to be a videographer, an artist, an author, and speaker. I really feel like I'm doing all those things in some measure. I only have one life; I don't want to die with regrets because I chose an easy path over what I was supposed to do.

Do you have more lives than one? Make the most of what you have. You're really, really need to do the job God has for you. You're not replaceable. He can tweak the plan, but you can choose to be John, the only disciple at the crucifixion, or Judas, the one who betrayed Jesus. Who'd you rather be? Even if you've had your Judas moments, it's not too late.

It might be the time to turn off the path that you've chosen for yourself and step into giving your life away. Not a lot of people choose to live this life because deep down we're not sure we trust that Jesus was telling the truth in Luke 9:24. We're not sure that if we lose our lives, we'll actually find them. We have good plans; surely God will just bless them. That's not the way it works though.

Consider the alternative life you could have, whether it's a life you could have planned for yourself or a life that God has. Consider what that life would look like and if you really want the life you have. Don't sugar-coat it. Don't make it worse than it would actually be either. Just think about that life and take the action you need to take to stay in God's will. A life in His will that looks horrible is still more fulfilling than one that is all about your plans, but looks easy. Choose well, my friends, and embrace the life you were meant to have. It's not too late.

20. Giving it All Away

When people think about giving, a lot of times they think about money. I agree that money is one of the things we can give. It's important to tithe and give money to your church. That's part of creating and being a part of a serving church. But don't comfort yourself that you're doing all God has for you if you don't put money in its proper place.

There was a time in my life where I looked at my bank account, I knew it would be tight to make it to pay day for food and we hadn't tithed. Sometimes when you're a writer starting a ministry, things can be tight. My wife looked at me and reminded me that despite our fights about money, we both said we'd tithe out of whatever we had. She was right, but I was scared. I didn't see how we were going to eat or buy gas. After some tense moments, we gave the check. The next week, I made more money than I'd made in the previous corporate job. Some of it didn't come in immediately, but I never missed a meal and our cars even had gas in them.

Something in me broke wide open that day. As I'm writing, it's Saturday, and we attend our church's Saturday service. After another tense discussion about money, I stopped a couple of paragraphs ago to ask my wife to write the tithe check. It was a somewhat lean week, but I'm convinced that just as Jesus saw the widow's mite as something to applaud, He'll applaud my tithe on my lean weeks as well as during the record ones.

I don't think He wants us to be generous with our money only. What if we should be generous with everything: our lives, our possessions, and our plans? Time greed is just as dangerous to your heart as money greed.

I wonder if the principle that I learned about giving money and letting God take care of your needs applies to time as well. I do know that the more I'm in charge of my time and attention, the more poorly it goes. When I strive to give who I am away, the results tend to be much more favorable.

We're all busy people. I don't think a lot of people wake up every day and think, "What will I do with all this time today?" I'm not foolish enough to believe that. I do think that you might have more time than you think you do. There are just some things that don't need to happen. I'm not one of those people who thinks television is inherently evil (I'm a videographer as well as an author), but television is one of the areas that you can cut from if you want to make room for the things you think are really important.

What can you cut? You've got stuff that you do out of habit that you might be fine with doing, but think of these things as time vampires that suck the life from your dreams and your service.

I'm not saying recreation should be at the top of the list; it shouldn't. God rested; Jesus rested. He created one of the Ten Commandments, on par with not killing by the way, that says to rest. Some things you're doing maybe aren't that fueling.

I've spent hours watching television shows I didn't like because "nothing else was on." I've slept in, not because I was tired, but because I could. I've done yard work, not to refuel myself or to keep a basic level of maintenance, but to impress the neighbors. Examine your motives and see if something doesn't fit with who you're supposed to be, and then find a way to cut it.

If you're doing something because your parents told you that "a man cuts his own grass" or "why would you hire a maid when you can do it yourself," maybe it's time to hire out some tasks to free up time for others. If it helps, the kid you hire to mow your lawn will appreciate the job as much as you'll appreciate the extra hour or more you get in return. Think about how freeing up your schedule can help others.

Sometimes, you have a tight schedule filled with important things. Have you ever considered taking time off of work or postponing a family vacation to help your church with an unusual event? What about thoroughly exhausting yourself for one or two days, so that God's plans can be advanced?

I'm not saying this should be the normal way you do things, but that sometimes you have to give everything you've got for a short time. Is your church opening a new building and it needs a bunch of people to help clean up in order to be done by opening weekend? Do you host a yearly event that takes a lot of work to pull off, especially in the last few days? Why not do whatever it takes to pull it off?

I'm not saying that you need to work yourself into an early grave, ignoring your family and treating your spouse like a stranger. I believe that God's calls aren't mutually exclusive. That means that if you're called to be a spouse and parent, there is no excuse to give up that calling for another calling.

The opposite is also true. If you're called to serve, and I think you are, your family is no excuse not to follow that calling. This isn't simple. You can't say, "I work 30% of the time, sleep 30%, spend 5% volunteering, and 25% with my family, with 10% for everything else." Sometimes you'll go over the top in one and the next week you'll spend extra time in the other.

You might be guessing that I'm not a great fan of "balance." I'm not. Jesus didn't live a "balanced life." Neither did Paul or the other Apostles. I don't see "live a balanced life" anywhere in the Bible. I don't think when Jesus said, "No one who puts a hand to the plow and looks back is fit for service in the kingdom of God," in Luke 9:62 that He meant "lead a balanced life." The context of that quote is that someone asked to bury his father before he followed Jesus. This quote was part of Jesus' response. That's not balanced.

I think there's something inside us that's drawing us toward something extreme. I don't want you to rob, kill, or destroy. That's not the type of extreme we're called to. I think we are called to giving our lives away because it's in service that we become who Jesus made us to be. Sometimes that's pleasant, nice, and easy. Sometimes, for a season, it looks like putting everything else aside, stepping out in faith, and doing what you know you're called to do even though you're sure you look a little crazy. If He's calling you to it, He's trustworthy. Lead your family so that they understand that they're part of a family that values sacrificing for the good of others. Make sure they understand that you love them. Then do what you're called to do, radically in service to others. You won't regret it.

21. You're Not Disqualified

If you're not conscious of how broken you are, if you don't know how bad you'd be without Jesus, it proves that you need Him all the more. You have so much pride that you dismiss the sins you commit. You likely don't easily ignore the ones others commit toward you. I don't think that applies to most people reading this though. I think most people have at least some sense of their own failure to consistently follow the plans of God.

I have had moments when I thought I'd so totally messed things up that there was no way God could still use me. You see, I know me. I know the dark thoughts that sometimes invade my mind. I know that I don't always dismiss them immediately.

I've been given the gift of seeing where I'd be without Him. It's not pretty. Left to my own plans, I'd stay a hermit, living my life totally online with little real human interaction. That's part of why He gave me a wife, so that I could be stretched and grown beyond hiding from the imagined slights and pain that I'd see outside my comfortable little world.

What about you? Do you ever see who you'd be without Him? Do you ever despair that parts of you just seem to stay broken, no matter how much you wish them to change? It's okay. I have.

I remember being in a prolonged season where I was stuck in a funk, for lack of a better term. My prayers seemed to go no farther than the ceiling. I kept thinking about how long I'd known Him and how little progress I'd made compared to where I thought I should be.

The apostle Paul was in a similar place, I think, when he wrote about the "thorn" in his flesh in 2 Corinthians 12:7b and following. He wrote about how it was something from Satan. It tormented him. He prayed over and over again for it to be gone. Sound familiar?

I don't know what has your number. I do know that something does. Is it an addiction? Is it control? How about pride? Maybe it's lust or greed. Whatever it is, you know that you hate it and love it at the same time. You hate the control it has over you, but you love something about it, so you give in over and over again.

In a situation like that, it's easy to feel like God can't or won't use you. It's easy to think that you've sinned away your potential. It's easy to think that you're just barely getting into heaven and only because of Jesus.

I tricked you a little bit there. No one earns a ticket to heaven. We've all earned a ticket to hell, but the fare to heaven can't be earned because it's already been paid. It can only be received as a gift from what Jesus did for us.

You probably know that, but do you *know* it? I knew I could trust God with my finances, in the moment where I didn't know where all the groceries between then and the next payday were coming from, I had to decide if I would know it intellectually or experientially. Those are totally different things. Once you've trusted God, even though you were right on the brink of really bad things happening, and He did what He said, it's easier to trust Him in other times.

Can you trust what the apostle Paul heard in his prayers? Can you trust that Jesus means, "My grace is sufficient for you; My power is made perfect in your weakness" (2 Corinthians 12:9)? What about Romans 8:1? Do you trust with your life that "There is therefore no condemnation for those who are in Christ Jesus?" That's a pretty verse, but look at the brokenness before it in Romans 7. The apostle Paul talks about wanting to do what's right and not being able to. Sound familiar?

God's grace covers all your sin. You aren't bad enough to be disqualified. You're not. Quit thinking, "Well, most people aren't, but I am!" Quit it. That's a lie! How do I know? I know me. I know that I don't deserve His grace and I don't deserve to be doing what I get to do. More than just me, I personally know a former stripper and adult entertainer who is starting a church in Miami with her husband. Before he married her, he was so surprised that the Bible had anything to say about premarital sex that I literally heard him yelling across a decent-sized house, "No! No! What do you mean? No!"

I know a recovering alcoholic whose addiction nearly cost her everything she held dear, but now leads a ministry where hundreds of addicts seek recovery every week.

I know a couple who were so close to divorce that he'd started saving up to pay the lawyer. After he and his wife not only decided not to get a divorce, but renewed their wedding vows. I was there for the ceremony. Later, he wrote a book about dating your spouse. Now they're leading other couples toward healing in their marriages.

Those stories might seem atypical today, but they're not atypical in the Bible. Don't forget that before Moses was a liberator, he was a murderer. Don't forget that the greatest king in Israel's history was also an adulterer and murderer. My namesake, the apostle Paul, persecuted the church and was a present, approving figure when the first Christian was martyred.

I brought up these three murderers because we think murder is worse than other sins. If you think these are the exceptions that prove the rule, what about Rahab the prostitute? What about Gideon, a man so scared that he was called into service while he was hiding for his life, threshing wheat in a winepress (where no one would look for it)?

Do I need to go on? I think it's clear that God wants you. He wants to have a relationship with you first. Don't get these backward. You do things for God as a result of your relationship with Him, not the other way around. He'd rather have you know Him than just do things for Him that you think are good things. Read Matthew 7:21-23 for more about people who get this one backwards.

Listen! If you know Him and He knows you, if your sins are forgiven, don't wallow in self-pity or guilt any longer. These are distractions. You can't get more forgiven by beating yourself up before you allow Jesus to forgive you. It's not Jesus' death on the cross **and** you being sad for days, weeks, months, or years. Be sorry, but don't let it keep you from what God has for you to do. That's the point of the feelings of disqualification you feel. The enemy wants you busy beating yourself up instead of helping others, loving people, and continuing Jesus' mission.

You are a beloved child of the Most High God because of what Jesus did to rescue you. That and only that is what qualifies Billy Graham, the apostle Paul, you, and me to serve Him and do His work. You need **nothing** else. Let the gratitude for that truth spill into how you serve, as someone who realizes the debt forgiven.

22. Letting Go of the Results

If you really, really care about what you're doing, it's easy to be so invested in the outcome that you can be hard to work with. If you think you're easy to be around with constant criticism, saying things like "they should have done what I told them," you're wrong. Think about how it feels when you're wrong and someone points it out. Hurts, doesn't it? You already knew your mistake, didn't you?

I know what it's like to be that guy because for years, I was him. I used to tell my leaders when they were going to make a mistake. I'd warn them while making it and I'd tell them that they should have listened to me after they made it. What's worse is that I would talk about them behind their backs and say things like "can you believe what they're doing?" This was wrong. It wasn't helping at all. In fact, it hurt people and hindered ministry.

One day I realized that even as one of the leaders in my church was learning to lead, she had to deal with me constantly pointing out her mistakes. I realized that I was causing her stress and grief, not because she was making mistakes, but because there was someone who seemed to always point them out. That's not love. That's not following well. That's not helpful to the mission at all. I'm happier now that I don't carry the weight of trying to always be right.

The world is much too complex for anyone to know the right answers all the time. Leaders get to shoulder the responsibility for making decisions and making mistakes in the process. They don't need people reminding them of those mistakes. They know about them.

When I started this ministry, I didn't know what I was doing. I still have a lot to learn, but I know that I need to keep making mistakes until I learn what I'm doing well enough to succeed. I heard a statistic today that 10% of American businesses fail every year. Last week, I heard Dave Ramsey say on the Entreleader podcast (http://www.daveramsey.com/entreleadership/podcast) that success is staying in business because so many fail. The church is like that. Don't be someone who helps your church fail. Help the other people on your team get back up when they make mistakes.

There are too many people that need to know about Jesus for churches who can reach them to fail. Expect that mistakes will be made, and be quick to brush them off and move on. That means that you should move on quickly, whether you made the mistakes or someone else did. Sometimes you need to debrief. Just pick the best time and place to do it.

Do everything you can to be someone who encourages those around you. People aren't perfect. No one knows all the answers. Sometimes you have to fail over and over and over again before you can succeed. Thomas Edison didn't invent the light bulb. Someone else did. He just figured out how to make a light bulb that was practical to manufacture and that lasted long enough to be useful. He was such a genius that he just knew immediately what … wait, no, he didn't. It took him failure after failure after failure before he realized what material the incandescent light bulb's filament should be made of and under what conditions it would work.

Think about your church that way. Your pastor and others at your church have a heart to see people come to know Christ (most do anyway). The problem is that people are complex. If you talk to a pastor in India who's been very successful in his ministry and one in Chicago with similar success, you'll get different advice on how to reach the people in your life that are far from God.

I think prayer gives us an edge in deciding the right course of action to take, but still we "see but a poor reflection as in a mirror" as the apostle Paul puts it in 1 Corinthians 13:12. Sometimes we're sure we hear God, but the results don't seem like ones we'd expect from Him. It happens all the time. That doesn't mean you're not a Christian. That means you made a mistake. Sometimes our own inner voices can sound like the Lord's still, small one.

Now that you know you make mistakes, extend grace to those who make decisions you can't control. It's possible that they weren't trying to ruin the church or cause failure. It's actually much more likely that they made a mistake just like you have.

If you hear something from God and you do it, you've done what you were supposed to do. Think about it. If Jesus says, "tell that person that I love them," and you do it, have you done what you were supposed to do? Yes, you have. What if they still make a bad decision afterward? Is that your fault? If you told them what you heard and did it with love, wanting the best for him or her, but they leave and take a drink after ten years of sobriety, do you blame yourself? You shouldn't. You did what you were supposed to do. Feel sad for the wrong decision and try to help the situation, but you're not responsible for other people's decisions.

Likewise, when you hear that you're supposed to tell your pastor something about the building campaign, if you tell him with good motives, wanting the best for the situation, you've done what you were supposed to do. If he decides that you heard wrong, which you may have, it's not your responsibility if something bad happens. Treat all your leader's decisions with grace. Be quick to forgive and make allowances for the fact that they're trying like you are. Each of us takes missteps. Remember this fact.

Your motivation in your interactions with people at church should always be to help and to follow the promptings of the Holy Spirit. Sometimes that means someone will listen to you and things will go better than they would have. It's possible that bad things will happen as a result of your advice too. Go forward in love in all you do.

This takes a kind of humility that's hard to cultivate. On one hand, have confidence in the words you share. Don't give advice from your own expertise, but only from what the Lord gives. Do it with open hands, not clutching what you heard as yours, but not requiring its use either. Recognize that you could be wrong, but that means you care enough to want to be right, so that you can be helpful and not so that you can be a superstar.

If you're operating in the right place with the right motives, you can forgive people who are doing the same when you don't agree. You should just want to see the Kingdom advance, to see lives and eternities change, to see God's will done. It doesn't matter who got to hear an idea that worked; it just matters that someone did and your church followed. It also doesn't matter who made the mistake; forgive and keep trying. Don't give up. People that my church will never reach are waiting on your church to reach them. Keep humbly trying to do His will and celebrate the successes while forgiving the failures.

23. Owner, but not Overlord

How invested are you in your church's mission? Are you waiting for a better thing to come along? Do you care, but not that much? Do you wake up on days you volunteer and thank God that you get to help? Do you think you could get God's mission accomplished if those around you would quit being so lazy and do what you tell them?

Spend a little time and honestly evaluate where you are. I'm looking for honesty here, not "I'm invested the right amount," when you know you're not. I'm not polling here. This is just for you.

To be completely clear, let me say it another way. Do you attend your church, but aren't involved? Are you involved, but only a little? Are you really involved? Is your church's mission, your mission? Will you do whatever it takes (and I mean whatever) to make sure that everyone does what they need to for the mission to be accomplished?

I'll share my answer, which might surprise you, given how radical some of the other chapters might have seemed so far. My church's mission is my mission. I'll stop short of answering the last question with "yes" though. There's a reason for that. I am responsible for me. I don't "lord authority" over anyone.

I want to help people grow and stretch, but each person answers for the decisions they make, not for the fact that as much as they tried, they couldn't get others to follow their ideas. I believe that we need to follow the directions of the Lord, but those directions always stop short of forcing others to agree with you or to do what you say.

Christian leadership isn't about coercion, but persuasion. The ends don't justify the means. The means matter. One should never hear, "I lied for the good of the Kingdom" or "I forced him to see my point of view like Jesus wanted." Even if you think these things without saying them, you're headed down a dangerous road.

It shows a lack of humility to think that you're the only one who can hear from God, or you're the only one trying really hard to follow Him. This was the mistake of the Crusades and the Inquisition. I'm sure people who actually heard from God tried to say we should persuade those who disagree, not kill them. Killing and torturing in Jesus' name are never viable means. Neither is deception or trickery. I don't think using a little-known procedural point in *Robert's Rules of Order* to get your way is right either. Sadly, I've seen too many churches trust rules based on Congressional interactions (like *Robert's Rules of Order* is) over the words of Christ.

One way to know that you've crossed the line is how much you use the word "they." Do you say, "I was trying to help the needy, but 'they' wouldn't let me," or "I was only doing what God told me to, but 'they' stopped me." I have a friend who says you should replace "they" with "my enemies" because that's what you really mean. It's harsh when "they" refers to people in your church that you claim to love, but try it. If you're using "they" this way, the sentence might sound harsh, but it's still true as you mean it.

When you feel this way, you're really questioning everyone's motives and attributing only bad ones to them. In psychology, this is called a "fundamental attribution error." If someone cuts you off in traffic, did they make a mistake, or is he a horrible driver who tried to kill you? If someone bumps into you in a crowd, did she lose his or her balance, or is she a pushy person? Most of the time your gut reaction tells more about you than it does about the person you're attributing malice to.

141

There are exceptions, but the church can't function on a snap judgment of malice. At a healthy church, you should attempt to assume the best of everyone. Practice looking for reasons why someone who is trying hard to follow Jesus would do what you just saw. What if you started with that thought and not the other? It could certainly change how you treat people.

I don't want you to slide toward apathy. Don't act like whatever people do doesn't matter; it does. God gives us things to do that matter. I don't understand why, because we mess them up so often, but He does. He also works in conjunction with our best efforts to accomplish His will.

Don't become paralyzed by fear either. I try to remember 2 Timothy 1:7 which says "For God did not give us a spirit of timidity, but a spirit of power, of love and of self-discipline." To me, that means that fear must either come from me or the devil. Either way, I want to interact with people out of love, boldness, and courage, not fear.

You can think of a million reasons not to ask someone to do something, but if that's who you're supposed to ask, then ask. Don't make a half-hearted, "You probably won't want to do it…" kind of request. Offer people the opportunity to be involved in the redemptive potential that you see in them. God turns shepherds into kings and murderers into missionaries.

He can turn a soccer mom into a leader or a self-employed dad into a force for good.

I want you to lead out of love. Love is the most potent tool in our toolbox. It treats others better than they treat themselves. It thinks of ways to ease burdens, and enable growth. Love isn't the infatuation of teens, but the power that caused the universe to be created. It was love that compelled Jesus to leave heaven and drove Him to the cross. Love is so inextricably a part of God that 1 John 4:8 says that "...God is love." It doesn't say that God has love or is in favor of love, but that He is love.

I know that some of you are reading this and wondering why you've read so far in this chapter. You think, "This chapter is about leading people. I'm not a leader." I actually doubt that. Only a few people possess absolutely no leadership. You might not lead groups, but leadership is little more than influence. If people ask your opinion, you have influence. If they do things the way you're doing them, you have influence.

The whole key to this chapter is not to misuse your influence, even if you think you're doing so for the good of the Kingdom of God. People matter much more than programs or strategies. People are the most important things to God. Every person is someone Jesus loves enough to die for.

Whether they accept that gift doesn't negate the fact that Jesus wanted them to receive it.

Influence them positively, not with threats or coercion. Those are your brothers and sisters. Some have been lost. Some were kidnapped. Some brainwashed. Some tortured. View difficult people through this lens: they were the kidnap victims, or were brainwashed or tortured at the hands of the enemy. They are not the enemy. You can't accomplish God's work if you treat people like they are.

God's will isn't for you to get your way. He doesn't want you to be the star of the show. He doesn't have any plans that involve you being rude or spiteful. The Holy Spirit isn't telling you to make people see why you're right. I'm sorry if you thought otherwise.

Treat your church's ministry like it's your own, but remember that it isn't. It belongs to God. He wants you to serve and love, not control and dominate. Each of us has a role to play, and each has direct access to God in order to learn about it. Let Him influence in the ways He wants. He loves the world much more than you do, so you can trust that His plans to save as many as He can don't need your domination to be completed. If you want to help, ask humbly and He'll let you.

24. Being Fed

"We're just looking for somewhere that we can be fed." I was talking with two of my favorite professors who were visiting my church when one of them said those words. "Being fed" is a Christian euphemism for going to a church with good, orthodox theology and biblically-based teaching. This is really something that people want so that they can grow in their faith and become more of who Jesus designed them to be.

I get the point of wanting to "be fed." You don't grow without food. You need more and more. There's just something about the phrase that doesn't sit well with me. I might be reading too much into it, but it just sounds too passive to me. I don't know who first came up with the phrase, but I wish they had used "eat fortifying spiritual food" instead of "be fed." Maybe they meant what they said, but I like to assume that it was just a turn of phrase and they didn't mean "I want to go to a church where I can passively receive without doing anything."

It really conjures up the image of a baby sitting with mouth open, waiting for formula or baby cereal. The parent scoops some up, puts it in her mouth, and all she has to do is swallow. It's very passive.

I think the "passive receiving" idea breeds some of the problems in American Christianity. It's easy to go "church shopping" as you look for the best place to "be fed." There's little more to it than looking for a new buffet or a better pizza. Notice that there's little, if any, value placed on relationships or service in that way of thinking. It's all about being served by people who are there to serve you. This is the opposite of the life Jesus talks about in Luke 22:26 when He says, "...the greatest among you should be like the youngest, and the one who rules like the one who serves."

I'm about to step on some toes. I hope yours are curling back in your shoes right now. I'm not aiming for the other guy, but to you if you've ever just wanted to be a recipient of teaching and not give back.

Service and putting others before yourself is what really leads to growth. Spiritually obese Christians who know all *about* the Bible, theology, and other "deep" subjects cause problems in the church if they don't serve. It's easy to pronounce someone a sinner who you think needs to reform if you're not in their life, seeing things from their point of view. When you see the struggles someone is going through, it's harder to judge their reactions.

I've come to believe that many prejudices are the result of assuming things that aren't true. We assume "fat people just need to exercise and eat right" or "unemployed people just need to go out and get a job." What if everyone that you look down on has tried what everyone says will work, as they understand it, and it hasn't worked for them? Instead, what if each of us were to get out of the pew and go toward service? Being a part of the lives of people, and caring for them instead of judging their category (fat, old, lazy, addict, etc.) will actually help others. The funny thing is that as you stretch, it actually helps you too.

Do you want to be better at evangelism? Taking classes, reading books, etc., will only help to a point. Jesus said, "Go into all the world…" in Mark 16:15, not take enough classes or read enough books. One verse really changed my outlook in this regard: Philemon verse 6 says "I pray that you may be active in sharing your faith, so that you will have a full understanding of every good thing we have in Christ." Did you see that? Look at the "so that." That refers to a result. The result is that you get "a full understanding of every good thing we have in Christ." What's the cause? It's being "active in sharing your faith."

Why are places like Africa and India so active evangelistically? The pastors and church members there don't have as much access to education as we do. They don't have eight Bibles on their living room shelves like I do (with more in my office). They share their faith, and as a result, they understand Christ and all He's done for us.

Evangelism is only one area where the "eat until you've grown enough" model is wrong. Think about all the attempts to help the poor. How many of these attempts are created by people who mean well, but who don't personally know anyone who is poor? I'm pretty sure that the members of Congress who are trying to fix these problems aren't socializing with the people they're trying to help, asking how they can actually help. Easing your conscience by writing a check once a month to your church to help the poor might not actually be getting the impact that it could if you went and volunteered your time to help. If you have money, it's easier to give it than to give your life, which is what serving is.

Maybe I'm writing to the wrong audience when I say these things. After all, you're reading a book on serving. Then again, you're *reading* a book on serving and maybe not actually serving. If you're gathering information so that someday you'll be good enough at having a servant's heart to actually serve selflessly, stop! Put this book down and take one small step into something that helps others. I'm not saying "Go start an orphanage in Africa" because that would probably be a mountain that's too large to climb. Some people need to start those orphanages. Others just need to spend some time at the Salvation Army. Maybe you need to quit avoiding people who are holding signs asking for help.

What little step can you take today to help someone else? Next time you're at the grocery store, if you see a stray cart in the parking lot, can you grab it and put it away? What about if you see a piece of trash on the ground? Can you pick it up and throw it away? Are you driving? Let someone in front of you in traffic. Are you getting ready to check out at the grocery store with a full cart? Let the person with five items in front of you in line. As you're leaving a store with change in your pocket, give it to any worthy cause, Christian or not (like disabled veterans), that happens to be collecting. Smile at people. Pay compliments like you're in a contest to see how many you can give. I sometimes hear James 4:17 in my head when I see a small way to help that no one will notice,

"Anyone, then, who knows the good he ought to do and doesn't do it, sins." I think small random acts of kindness ought to mark our lives.

These are small ways to go about serving. Don't stop there. Volunteer at a shelter. Cook for an AA meeting. Stop by a firehouse with a pot of chili. Every time there's an opportunity to serve at church, try to help out. Give to special offerings. Host missionaries or others in your home.

Service is the exercise in any Christian's life. If you stop at being fed, you'll get fat. After you exercise, you're more likely to eat the healthy food in front of you than to wait for the fattening, so-called "deep teaching." Don't let knowledge puff up; let love build up. I want your heart to be strong, able to love the unlovable, willing to take a risk on those who will likely break it. That's what you get from service: a more loving heart.

25. Serving Outside of Church

Right after I got married, I got a job at a restaurant as a server. I always tried to do my best and to interact with the other servers in a way that would show them Jesus. I tried not to work on Sundays. They told me that I could have Sundays off if I took less desirable shifts. That turned out not to be the case, so I eventually left. I'd often take care of people in suits and dresses who were obviously there after church. Much to my chagrin, the work I'd been doing to show Jesus to the servers around me was undone every week by the people who came to the restaurant after church.

Time and again, good servers would get 6-10% tips after doing a great job. I began to pray that I'd get the "cheap Christians" instead of those who didn't need another reason to stay away from church. It hurt me to watch it happen; I began to wonder why.

One time in particular, an older couple came in and were seated. I watched as they prayed for their food and made sure not to interrupt. At the end of the meal, they handed me a tip along with a tract and said, "You can have this," indicating the money, "if you promise to read this," indicating the tract. I thanked them and told them that I'd known Jesus for nearly twenty years and that I was, in fact, in seminary. They kept the tract and said, "We knew something was different about you."

I wanted to cry. They had offered me 10% of the bill (less than $2) for my soul. Happily, I'd given it to Jesus years before. I spent a moment praying, thanking God that He'd entrusted me with the work of blocking the people around me from well-meaning, but clueless people.

You may say, "Paul, maybe that's all they had." That's true. As a man who has had so little in my life that I've left one place and prayed for enough gas to get home, or who has tithed even though I didn't know where money was coming from to feed my family, I choose to eat in restaurants where I can afford to treat the serving staff like they really matter, not like they don't.

One time, I received an inheritance from a cousin who'd died childless. I went to a place to eat after church. My church is casual, so I don't wear a suit, but I often wear t-shirts with our logo on them. When the bill came, I realized that they'd removed my daughters' meals. The special that day was that kids ate free. To try and be frugal, I'd ordered water, so my bill was less than $10 for all three of us. I decided to tip 100%. Why so much? It was about what I'd entered the restaurant planning to spend. Since my wife had a meeting and my daughters' meals were free, it seemed right to spend a few dollars more than I felt obligated to, to show appreciation to the guy who waited on us. I didn't give him a tract. I didn't invite him to church. I just treated him well.

This past August, my church did a week of "Random Acts of Kindness." We gave gifts to sanitation workers. We took a roasted pig to a fire station. We took snacks to teachers in every school in the city. We didn't advertise the church, but simply said that we wanted them to feel appreciated.

Showing up to an event en masse with church shirts, handing out a pamphlet and some small gift so they'll take it isn't service; it's advertising. In its time, done right, there's nothing wrong with it, but don't comfort yourself thinking that you're serving someone if your motivation is just to get more people to your church. Loving people should be the purpose of serving them, not the means to grow your influence.

I actually prefer not to do things that anyone can identify, if they notice at all. If you're walking down a city street and see an expired meter, why not add a nickel or a quarter? If you see a piece of trash, pick it up. If someone needs help, then help.

I was taught that you shouldn't help people begging for money because they "might not use it right." While that's true, I don't see that in the Bible. In fact, I see Jesus helping people all the time. When you help someone in any way, it's possible they'll misuse your gift. Suppose you stop to help change a tire. The person can easily hop back in the car and drive to rob a bank. If you tell someone they look good in a blue shirt, they might wear that blue shirt to find someone to cheat on their spouse with. You're not responsible for bad choices people make as a result of a good thing you do. So, take care of the poor and sick like Jesus did. Treat people like they matter to you like they matter to Jesus.

Don't let service stop when you leave church. Let it overflow from the gratitude that you have for what Jesus saved you from. What good things can you do today? How can you raise the level of kindness in your city?

Think of what the world would look like if all Christians, everywhere, believed that how we treat others reveals our love for Jesus. What if "Christian" became synonymous with "generous, selfless, kind, and loving" instead of "hypocritical and judgmental"? I'd love to live in a world where people assumed that a kind gesture must have been done by a Christian. I want to see people asking why you're doing something to serve them and not assume you're selling something.

Above all, the more "Christian" you look, the more you need to assume that people are watching. I keep bumper stickers to a minimum on my car because I'm not as good a driver as my wife is, and I don't want people cursing Jesus because of my mistakes. I don't drive aggressively, but I do sometimes make mistakes that I'd prefer to take the wrath for. At the same job where I was offered a tract, one of the cooks came out after the shift was done and all the servers were sitting around. He started talking about being cut off and flipped off by someone in a van with "one of those Jesus fishes" on it. As he passed the van on the other side, the passenger rolled down her window and yelled "Jesus loves you."

We can do better. For the most part, people I talk to don't bring up the Crusades or the Inquisition when they talk about Christian hypocrisy. They talk about their experiences, about ways that we could help their perceptions, but don't. Even if the people you talk to bring up these sad times in history, we can change perceptions by what we do today. I wish we could blow their expectations away. Have you ever dreaded calling a large corporation, but the customer service is so good that not only are you surprised, but you tell all your friends? Apple has done that for me more than once. Think of everything you do outside of church as service to the people who might someday know Jesus if they see His love in you. We're His ambassadors. We're his customer service and sales team. Treating them badly says, "we don't want you" and by implication, Jesus doesn't either.

Let's do everything we can to raise expectations. Let's treat each and every person we meet like someone valuable enough that Jesus would have just died for them, because He did.

And so it begins...

About the Author

Paul Alan Clifford (December 19, 1973-) was born in Louisville, Kentucky to parents who thought that they couldn't have children. He grew up with the thought that he was meant to do something unusual with his life. This unwavering feeling led him to seminary where he learned that his interest in technology could be used by God.

He married his beautiful wife, Christina, in 1999 with whom he raises their two daughters, Trinity and Eliana. He founded TrinityDigitalMedia.com in February of 2011 to fulfill his dream to give his life away to the Acts 2 vision of the Church -- bringing people to know the forgiveness and love of Jesus.

Would your prefer ebook?

Just go to http://TrinityDigitalMedia.com/The-Serving-Church-Free, give me your email address, and I'll send you the eBook versions for Kindle, iBooks, Nook, and PDF for FREE. Hurry, offer ends 12/31/2013.

For more information about appearance and Paul's latest projects, join his newsletter at: TrinityDigitalMedia.com/newsletter

Made in the USA
Charleston, SC
25 July 2015